DEMOCRACY WITHOUT
NATIONS?

CROSSCURRENTS

ISI Books' Crosscurrents series makes available in English, usually for the first time, new translations of both classic and contemporary works by authors working within, or with crucial importance for, the conservative, religious, and humanist intellectual traditions.

DEMOCRACY WITHOUT NATIONS?

THE FATE OF SELF-GOVERNMENT IN EUROPE

Pierre Manent

TRANSLATED FROM THE FRENCH BY
Paul Seaton

ISI
BOOKS

WILMINGTON, DELAWARE

Manent, Pierre.

    Democracy without nations? : : the fate of self-government in Europe / Pierre Manent ; translated from the French by Paul Seaton. —1st American ed. —Wilmington, Del. : ISI Books, 2007.

        p. ; cm.
        (Crosscurrents)

        ISBN: 978-1-610170-84-0

        Translation of: La raison des nations : réflexions sur la démocratie en Europe. Paris: Gallimard, 2006.
        Includes index.

    1. National state. 2. European federation. 3. Democracy—Europe. 4. Religion and politics—Europe. I. Seaton, Paul, 1954– I. Title. II. Raison des nations. English. III. Series: Crosscurrents (Wilmington, Del.).

JC311 .M332513 2007   2007933851
320.54/094—dc22   0711

Originally published (without appendices) as:

La raison des nations: Réflexions sur la démocratie en Europe
de Pierre Manent
World copyright © Editions GALLIMARD, Paris, 2006

English translation published in the United States by:

ISI Books
Intercollegiate Studies Institute
3901 Centerville Road
Wilmington, DE 19807
www.isibooks.org
Manufactured in the United States of America

CONTENTS

TRANSLATOR'S INTRODUCTION

PIERRE MANENT HAS written that Charles de Gaulle was the last French statesman who knew how to speak to France about herself. Among political philosophers, the same could be said about Manent, who writes analytically and synthetically, even lyrically, about France. For three decades he has explored the complex relationship between the nation and democracy, between representative government and partisanship. His writings judiciously combine description and analysis, criticism and constructive counsel.

We Americans can learn much from him—and not just about his native France or contemporary Europe. Manent is perhaps the ablest defender of the nation-state, and perhaps the most incisive philosophical student of politics, writing today. Since America is not only the democratic political community par excellence but also a nation-state whose citizens are quite attached to this particular form, these subjects must be of great concern to us. Tocqueville said that in writing *Democracy in America* he thought of France as he penned each page. The American reader is likely to return the favor when reading this latter-day Tocqueville's analysis of contemporary France and Europe.

Manent's central themes were already present in his first books (those which appeared between 1977 and 1987). Then as now, he was primarily concerned with "liberalism" or liberal democracy, the nation, and what he calls "the political nature of man and the political condition of mankind." Approaching these topics dialectically, Manent combines readings of eminent political thinkers with a distinctive conception of political philosophy itself. After gaining a reputation as a brilliant expositor of texts, around 1993 he began to speak more directly in his own voice. And with his important books at the beginning of this century he has cemented his reputation as a first-rank philosophical analyst of contemporary political life.

His first four books were aptly titled *Naissances de la politique moderne: Machiavel, Hobbes, Rousseau* (1977); *Tocqueville and the Nature of Democracy* (1982; 1996 English translation); *An Intellectual History of Liberalism* (1987; 1996 English translation); and *Les libéraux* (1986). The last volume was a hefty anthology of twenty-three broadly "liberal" thinkers, from John Milton to Bertrand de Jouvenel, who had made the relationship between "power and liberty" their focal concern. (In Europe, of course, the word *liberal* is roughly akin to the term *classical liberal* in America.)

As the titles of these books indicate, Manent's broad focus during these years was modern politics, with special attention given to liberalism and modern democracy. Liberalism originally was a distinctive body of doctrines and set of social and political institutions that construed man as a free individual. It intended government to protect man and his manifold freedoms, not to dictate to him in the name of a sovereign good. It eventually evolved into a specific form of democracy—precisely "liberal democracy"—based on the free individual and the institutionalization of popular sovereignty (a sovereignty usually accompanied by appropriate limits, checks, and balances).

After the initial development of liberal democracy in the late eighteenth and early nineteenth centuries, a second wave of "conservative-minded" liberal thinkers emerged, including François Guizot and Benjamin Constant. Contemplating the French Revolution and its works, they discovered dangerous potentials and important defects in earlier liberal theory and democratic practice and sought to address them, all the while remaining committed to "modern liberty." Their most penetrating theorist was Alexis de Tocqueville, whom Manent calls "indispensable" for understanding modern democracy. Manent's 1982 book, *Tocqueville and the Nature of Democracy*, now a widely recognized classic in Tocqueville scholarship, draws deeply from the Tocquevillean tradition of chastened liberalism.

Manent's 1986 anthology exemplified—and its preface titled "The Situation of Liberalism" nicely summed up—his Cold War–era investigations. Here he argued that liberalism's admirable domestic arrangements, especially its openness to a variety of conflicting opinions, made it difficult for its adherents to recognize the true nature of Communist "ideocracies"—regimes based upon the fundamentally mendacious Communist ideology—as the mortal antagonists they were. In general, liberalism tended to give short shrift to the political dimensions of reality and to dim "the civic instinct" of modern men and women.

Liberalism also had helped produce a general situation in which liberal democracy's traditional political framework, the sovereign state and the nation, was weakened. Both globalization abroad and economism at home called into question the sovereign nation and its capacity for independent action. These were worrisome developments already evident in the latter stages of the Cold War. Then came the collapse of communism and a new situation for the West's liberal democracies, one that called for fresh thinking and new emphases.

Manent's new concerns were previewed in a 1993 talk he gave in Munich. In this speech titled "De Gaulle: The Nation as Object of Thought and Action," Manent retraced the quintessential Frenchman's reflections on the nation, especially his beloved France. He used these Franco-focused reflections, however, to illuminate the situation in which the reunified German nation found itself. The status of the nation was a common European problematic.

At about this time the Maastricht Treaty was ratified, which transformed the European Community into the European Union and was intended as an important step toward the full unification of Europe. This was a major event in the postwar life of European nations, a revealing conjunction of the "statics and dynamics"—the structural features and dominant tendencies—of the contemporary European scene.

As a political philosopher, Manent could not but be fascinated by this new political organization. Indeed, he asked, *was* it genuinely political? With this question we come to one of the most fundamental of Manent's central themes. In his judgment, many contemporary Europeans believe that they either are beyond politics (the "postpolitical illusion") or can dispense with it (the "antipolitical temptation"). This has been one of the chief subjects of his recent work, beginning with *A World beyond Politics? A Defense of the Nation-State* (2001; 2006 English translation).

An illusion is "a representation of the world, tied to a desire," writes Manent. In the name of the sovereign individual and of a totally unified humanity, contemporary European democratic humanitarianism envisages and acts as if a postpolitical order has been attained in Europe and in principle is within sight *dans le monde entier*. In America, we recognize this same mind-set at work in the phenomena of political correctness and multiculturalism and in the underlying ideology of transnational progressivism. Absolutizing relativism, yet tempered by egalitarianism, this view is made plausible by the denial of any intractable "significant human differences." Many have criticized this antipolitical position, but few, if any, have provided as philosophically penetrating an analysis as has Manent.

THE PRESENT VOLUME contains three Manent *écrits*. The heart of the volume consists of a translation of Manent's most recent work, titled in French *La raison des nations: réflections sur la démocratie en Europe* (Gallimard, 2006). In this elegant work he describes and subjects to critical scrutiny "an immense phenomenon" at once ideological and intimate. Fundamentally, this phenomenon consists of certain "ideas"—about democracy, about Europe—that pervade the European continent and are being employed to reshape it and its inhabitants. These ideas are strengthened by certain emphatically democratic passions found in many Western hearts. Both these ideas and these passions are given shape by a particular "advanced" or "progressive" conception of democracy that Manent calls "pure democracy." This idea of democracy is troublingly apolitical. Indeed, it is being increasingly severed from "democracy in the original, that is, political sense of the term." Before the idea of pure democracy the old democratic political instruments of the sovereign state and representative government are asked, or compelled, to bow; within the purview of pure democracy, the nation—another name for the people—has no authoritative standing.

As the French title of the work—the "reason" or *raison d'être* of nations—indicates, Manent's goal is to provide a specifically political defense of democracy's older meaning and supporting framework. This does not mean that he is simply a "Euroskeptic." He is fully open to the construction of a Europe that would take its place as an actor on the world stage. But any Europe that is worth pursuing must recognize the political requirements of the human world while affording individuals the means to be democratic citizens. It must also appropriately respect and engage "the old nations."

The appendices of the present volume contain two pieces that appeared at an interval of slightly more than a decade. Appendix A (which also provides the name of the volume as a whole) consists of a 1996 article titled "Democracy without Nations?" in which Manent first traced the "ambiguity" haunting the construction of

Europe. Was Europe to be a new "political body," one in which contemporary Europeans could effectively exercise their democratic vocation as self-governing citizens and their natures as political animals? Or would it become an ever-expanding "network" of communications and commerce, a modern-day Alexandrine cultural bazaar, a realm of tenderly—or aggressively—protected human rights that nevertheless lacked the requisite instruments for collective deliberation and decision, for common defense and action?

At the time, Manent left the question open. But even in 1996 he argued both for the indispensability of some definite "political form" for any viable Europe and for a more positive consideration of the traditional nation. After all, the nation was modern Europe's own invention, a remarkable "concrete universal" that had enabled its denizens fruitfully "to put in common speeches and actions" (Aristotle's phrase in the *Nicomachean Ethics,* which Manent loves to cite). As such, the nation merits serious consideration, especially by thoroughgoing democratic spirits who are tempted to think that they—and democracy itself—are self-sufficient, that they are the sovereign masters of themselves and of existence. In Manent's judgment, more than a little hubris has characterized European democracy during the past few decades.

In the last part of *La raison des nations* and throughout the final piece in this volume (Appendix B: "What Is a Nation?"), Manent discusses religion, especially (but not solely) the Christian religion. In Manent's view, reflecting on Christianity is indispensable to his exploration of the relationship between the nation and democracy. On the one hand, Manent seeks to understand the distinctive course of European political history, which first produced "the Christian kingdom" and the nation-state, then the modern democratic nation-state, and now risks abandoning the nation-state and radically transforming democracy itself. "Everyone" knows that Europe's *Sonderweg*—its special path—is unintelligible apart from Christianity. Not everyone, however, has been as persistent as Manent in investigating and coming to terms with this massive fact. Few have been as emphatic as he in affirming Christianity's essential contribution to the political career—as well as the spiritual and moral substance—of Europe. On the other hand, Manent also wants to consider religion's presence on the contemporary scene insofar as it bears upon political matters. In conducting his analyses, however, Manent has to challenge certain contemporary intellectual habits.

As valuable and even indispensable as "our liberal arrangements" may be, including the separation of church and state, as a "rule of our actions" they should not simply govern our thought about religion and politics. Nor should we merely consider religion as a matter of individual choice or rights. There is something manifestly public about religion, says Manent. It is an objective phenomenon available for description and analysis. We must trust our own eyes "for once"—instead of liberal categories and prejudices—in order to come to terms with it.

If we do, we will see that religion and politics constantly overlap, that they are not completely separable. This should come as no surprise, says Manent, because both are forms of human "communion." With this last term we come to perhaps Manent's deepest theme. One learns from Aristotle that *koinonia,* "community" or holding-in-common, is central to understanding politics and to the realization of our natures as rational and political animals. One learns from St. Paul and St. Augustine that the Christian church understands itself as a new and even deeper community, a *communio.* The French poet and philosopher Charles Péguy (1876–1914) drew from both traditions in considering the *mystiques* or "communions" constituting the nation, the church, and the synagogue. Manent has studied and learned from each of these thinkers in developing his own distinctive perspective.

Manent convincingly describes his contemporaries as hyper-democratic. They tend to believe that what they have in common is adequately defined by individual rights, shared instruments of communication, and whatever material and cultural goods they choose to identify with or exchange Once upon a time, their common goods may have included religion and the nation, but no longer. Manent seeks to convince his contemporaries that their current arrangements are less than adequate—indeed, that as individuals they are less self-sufficient than they believe. He likewise seeks to indicate ways in which their secular categories of self-understanding fail to recognize important dimensions of European reality. Having done so, he can advise them. Democracy's promise of human community, of mutual respect for our shared humanity and the opportunity to fully develop it, is much richer as well as more demanding than they imagine.

In a parting aphorism, Manent declares that democratic freedom, "consent," must seek "communion" if democracy is to fulfill its promise for humanity. This "must" implies a "can." His entire oeuvre points toward ways that contemporary democratic man can and ought to strive to achieve that humanizing conjunction of freedom and political—as well as spiritual—community.

I WISH TO thank Pierre Manent for his many acts of friendship and for the pleasures involved in engaging with his thought. I thank Daniel J. Mahoney for introducing me to Manent and his work. Dan has been an endless source of counsel, assistance, and bibliographical references. Finally, I thank my parents, Pete and Nancy, for life and their unfailing support.

Paul Seaton
Baltimore, Maryland
August 2007

LA RAISON DES NATIONS

FOREWORD

I OWE THE reader an explanation concerning the character of this little book. For thirty years I have devoted myself to the study of political philosophers. It seemed to me that their works shed the most light on our life as citizens. If Montesquieu already provided the most convincing description of the role of parties in a system of representative government, if Tocqueville already penetrated most profoundly into the life and movement of democracy, then one best understands the things themselves by reading them as carefully as possible. This at least has been my experience. Therefore, up to now I have written only in order better to understand those I read, and to help those who read my work do the same.

This book is different. It is not that, worn out by my exhaustive studies, I suddenly decided to enter into the civic conversation and empty my quiver, so to speak. These pages are in fact the condensation of much intellectual work. That work was sparked by the almost painful recognition of a phenomenon that is at once immense and penetrates into the depths of each one of us. If the desire to publish this inquiry overcame other reasons urging not to do so, it is because I had the notion—the reader will forgive me this thought!—that this phenomenon increasingly eludes our shared awareness even as it grows apace. But here however, the political philosophers are not directly helpful and so I have had to strike out on my own.

The phenomenon to which I refer is the erosion—perhaps even the dismantling—of the political form that for so many centuries has sheltered the endeavors of European man. I refer to the nation. A political form—the nation, the city—is not a light overcoat that one can put on and take off at will and still remain what one is. It is the Whole within which all the elements of our life come together and take on meaning. If our nation *suddenly* disappeared and its bonds were dispersed, each of us immediately would become a stranger, a monster, to himself. Those who believe the most that they are the most emancipated from their nation still live largely from its fecundity. But how difficult it is to describe the nation and its effects!

This, however, is what I attempt to do in the following pages. By means I would not normally recommend in that this work follows no particular method, I attempt to enter into the long process—one rich in metamorphoses—by which the European nation was constructed and then began to deconstruct. These metamorphoses have been slow but also violent. They have stretched the strings of our souls to the breaking point. Any analysis that seeks to be faithful to them cannot fail to evince a certain abruptness from time to time. The reader is forewarned.

Let me give one last indication of what lies ahead. Religion—or religions—occupies a large place in these pages. The reader will perhaps be surprised. If the separation of church and state is precious as a rule of our actions, it becomes ruinous if we make it the rule of our thought. Politics and religion are never entirely separate or separable. One cannot understand either, therefore, unless one takes them together.

THE PRESENT SITUATION

If everyone does not feel what I am talking about, I am wrong.
—Montesquieu

THE REFLECTIONS PRESENTED to the reader are, I fear, far removed from common opinion. Today, all of us—at least in Europe—are moved and even carried away by an idea that is also a sentiment and even a passion: the idea that humanity is proceeding toward its necessary unification. The "sentiment of resemblance" which Tocqueville already saw as the central emotion of human beings in democracies has become a *passion* for resemblance. It is no longer simply a matter of recognizing and respecting the humanity of each human being. We are required to see *the other* as *the same as ourselves*. And if we cannot stop ourselves from perceiving what is different about him, we reproach ourselves for doing so, as if it were a sin. But what can "same" or even "similar" mean to someone who refuses to see what is different? Vaguely perceiving differences they really do not want to see, and thus see with a great deal of pain,

Europeans immerse themselves in an *indifference* toward the world that their humanitarian endeavors hide less and less well.

We learn to see what is similar and different in the context in which we experience these qualities—that is to say, first of all, in the *political body* to which we belong. For Europeans, for centuries this body has been the nation-state. This political form weaves together what is similar and different in particularly complex and subtle ways. Beyond its borders, each nation saw in the neighboring nation both a partner and a rival it sought to best in works of war and peace. But in truth, it shared these works in common with the other. Each nation raised its voice—its propositions on humanity—in the "European concert." Internally, class struggles troubled each nation even as they gave birth, sometimes violently, to its unity. In short, it was across the differences of nation and class that we sought and exercised our common humanity.

The weakening of the European nations weakens this framework in which the similar and the different can be recognized and take on meaning. It is not surprising, therefore, that we seek refuge in a vague idea of human unity, an imminent unity that would resolve by a kind of internal necessity the problem of human order we no longer know how to state. This idea takes rather different forms depending upon whether one looks at "old Europe" or its cross-Atlantic progeny. But if European quietism presents a vivid contrast to American activism, the two are nonetheless versions of what one might call "democratic empire." Both sides propose such an empire with equal conviction and even obstinacy.

THE AMERICAN VERSION of empire manifests the following traits. One central nation, the model and guardian of democracy, encourages all peoples, whoever and wherever they are, to establish a democratic regime and cultivate democratic mores. After all, democracy is natural to man. One discerns on the horizon a world made up of democratic nations; among them, the rules and regulations of commerce and human rights compose an ever-tighter network of relations that enhance world unity every day. And if a "rogue state," moved by the hatred evil reserves for the good, seeks to trouble this natural harmony, then the awesome military superiority of America will arrest the rebel and punish the criminal. The American version of democratic empire is characterized by a harmonious mixture of older elements, such as the maintenance of nations and willingness to take recourse to force, with newer elements. The primary newer element is the vision of a united world in which collective differences will no longer be truly meaningful or significant.

The European version of democratic empire presents other traits. Its center is not a central nation but what I will call a central human *agency*. This agency was born (since everything has to be born someplace) on either side of the Rhine. But it soon detached itself from any particular territory or people and is now occupied with extending the area of "pure democracy." Pure democracy is democracy without a people—that is, democratic *governance*, which is very respectful of human rights but detached from any collective deliberation. The European version of democratic empire distinguishes itself by the radicality with which it detaches democracy from every real people and constructs a *kratos* without a *dèmos*. What now possesses *kratos* is the very idea of democracy. The European empire, however, has one thing in common with the American version: it too is animated by a vision of a world in which no collective difference is significant.

Europeans and Americans are therefore separated despite sharing the same idea of the world—albeit of a different color—in important respects. The explosion of human unity makes both groups less capable of actually seeing the present state of the world. Occupied with building our twin towers of Babel, we no longer appreciate the fact that separations between and among human groups cannot be entirely overcome. Nor do we see that this fortunate impotence is the condition of human liberty and diversity.

THE TWO VERSIONS of the democratic movement are marked by the same dizziness, even giddiness, before number (or quantity) and spatial extension. The "global middle class" is constructed in units of hundreds of millions. It is composed of those who can master the new instruments of communication and have the capacity to quickly adapt to the rules of good governance. At the beginning of a new century, the diffusion of rules and regulations provides a substitute for the reality and energies of collective willing. On the one hand, there is the indefinite extension of "the construction of Europe." On the other, there is the American policy of "global democratization."

This indefinite spatial extension is accompanied, especially in Europe, by an extraordinary temporal retrenchment. The past is deemed culpable, made up of collective crimes and unjustifiable constraints. As more and more populations are added to the immense "global middle class," each people is commanded to divorce itself from its culpable past—one said to be defined by intolerance and oppression. At the same time the monuments of their crimes, whether cathedrals or pyramids, are enlisted as elements of a "global patrimony."

But how can one simultaneously condemn all pasts and recognize all cultures? Since every *significant* collective difference puts human unity in danger, one must render every difference *insignificant*. Thus, aspects of the most barbarous past become elements of an infinitely respectable "culture," since the only truly evil thing today is to think and act according to the idea that one form of life is better than another. To summarize our condition and conviction: the only blameworthy human conduct for us is what used to be called "conversion." In this way, our extreme democracy, enjoining absolute respect for "identities," joins hands with the fundamentalisms that punish apostasy with death. There is no longer any legitimate transformation or change of mind, because no one preference is more legitimate than any other. Under a flashing neon sign proclaiming "human unity," contemporary

Europeans would have humanity arrest all intellectual or spiritual movement in order to conduct a continual, interminable liturgy of self-adoration.

NOT TOO LONG ago, the democratic idea justified and nourished the love each people naturally has for itself. But now, in the name of democracy, this love is criticized and mocked. What happened? And what future can human *association* have if no particular group, no "communion," no people is legitimate any longer? What becomes of us if only human *generality* is legitimate?

It is amazing to see how quickly the meaning of the democratic nation has been lost in Europe—the very place where this extraordinary form of human association first appeared!

The democratic nation tied the democratic future of a people to its monarchical or feudal past. The mores of the democratic present introduced whole peoples to a wider and deeper communion. The "barbarous" past itself was redeemed by the free present, as well as by a future that was bound to be even freer. The present generation was seen as the latest advancing wave arising from previous generations. It joined the immemorial past with the indefinite future; it thus placed the present under the double authority or solicitation of these two. In this light, one can see that Ernest Renan's famous formula stating that the nation is a "daily plebiscite" failed accurately to identify the nation—as he had aimed to do with his 1882 address, "What Is a Nation?" Each "day" of the nation is connected with its origins long past as well as its open, indefinite future. Each day of the nation connects the three dimensions of time. The warp and woof of a nation's time is finely textured.

This in no way contradicts freedom, since no one—whether an individual or even an institution—wholly contains the nation's time. Only political liberty offers the possibility of responding to the double solicitude of the past and the future in their inconquerable amplitude. It is well known that the European nation was extremely meticulous when it came to matters of space and territory. We ought not to overlook how much the nation helped us to inhabit time and hold together—with equal zeal—past, present, and future.

Today, however, this unifying principle of our lives has lost its connective force. The elements it had held together are now rediscovering their independence. As a result, we celebrate the arrival of a brighter future even as significant meaning retreats into elements of the past—into "regions" and "religion." By stripping the nation of its legitimacy the contemporary democratic movement brings predemocratic "communions" to the fore. But the democratic nation was the mediation of mediations, bringing together consent and communion. How can we continue to live without such mediation? What human association, old or new, will be able to bring consent and communion together in a viable way?

DEMOCRACY

I HAVE JUST spoken of *the* democratic movement. Today we speak of "democracy" in the singular. In this sense, popular usage joins scholarly discourse. And both join Tocqueville, who presented democracy as an immense phenomenon that came from afar and is leading us toward unknown shores, but also as remaining essentially the same throughout its long development. According to Tocqueville, democracy is first and foremost "the equality of conditions." The democratic movement is a movement toward an ever-greater equality of conditions.

Thirty years ago our manner of speaking about democracy was different. The substantive "democracy" was usually accompanied by an adjective. One spoke of "liberal" or "bourgeois" democracy, of "socialist" or "popular" democracy. Scholarly opinion very much doubted that there was something called democracy *tout court*.

These changes in popular and academic discourse invite us to begin our inquiry into the European nation by attempting to retrace the movement of democracy in the main lines of its history, or at least to discover the rhythm of that movement. Inquiring after the various ways in which the question of democracy has been posed, we can see how it came to the point where it finds itself today.

THE TWO DATES most generally acknowledged to have structured or punctuated the development of modern European democracy are separated by more than a century: 1848 and 1968.

1848 was the year of the *Communist Manifesto* and those bloody June days in Paris when the National Guard crushed the Paris workers' uprising—one the closing of the national workshops had provoked. In short, 1848 was the initial explosion of *the social question*, the declaration of class warfare, and the establishment of class struggle.

Let us recall what happened in 1968. We can recall it because we were there; and some even took part in the last burst of the torch that had first been lit in 1848. Recall the Marxist consensus; the bourgeoisie up against the wall once again; their hands again white on the factory doors; Sartre on his barrel; and Raymond Aron holding the mirror of Flaubert's *Sentimental Education* up to "the elusive Revolution."[1]

From 1848 to 1968: it seems to me that we have here the axial core, the inner circle—the *magma*, one might say—of our modern history. Then, *the* problem of democracy was called "the social question." It was Marx who posed this question in the fullest and most radical manner.

Democracy, however, did not come into existence in 1848. In the 1820s it was already "at the point of overflowing its banks" (as the French Doctrinaires put it). The greatest book ever written on democracy was published in 1835 and 1840. Tocqueville organized

---

1. Manent alludes to Raymond Aron, *La Révolution introuvable: Réflexions sur la revolution de Mai (1968)* (Paris: Fayard, 1968); English language edition: *The Elusive Revolution: Anatomy of a Student Revolt* (New York: Praeger, 1969). In this work Aron wrote about the events and "spirit" of 1968 in a vein comparable to the one in which Flaubert and Tocqueville wrote on the revolution of 1848. (Trans.)

his *Democracy in America* around a double comparison. One axis of *Democracy in America* compares French democracy with American democracy, or the French Revolution with the American Revolution. The other axis compares democracy in general with the social form that preceded it, what Tocqueville calls "aristocracy." When did modern democracy begin? In any account, it appeared along with the American Revolution; let us then say in 1776, the date of the Declaration of Independence. How can we define this "Tocquevillean" period synthetically? Its problem was not the social question but rather the actualization, the institutionalization, of the new legitimizing principle of the sovereignty of the people. According to Tocqueville, the great difference between France and the United States lay in their differing modes of institutionalizing that principle.

But how do these two great periods connect? The period that opened in 1848 might be understood as refuting Tocqueville's perspective. As I have said, for Tocqueville, democracy primarily means "the equality of conditions." The emergence of the social question entailed the observation that at the heart of the new society reigned, not an equality of conditions, but a new *inequality* of conditions. In Tocquevillean language this is the anti-Tocquevillean meaning of 1848. Tocqueville the political actor became a government minister just as Tocqueville the political thinker appeared to have been decisively refuted. But 1968 represented Tocqueville's revenge. By an irony marking the inverse of what had happened in 1848, the end of the social question announced itself in the guise of a Marxist consensus. And with that end came the return of a Tocquevillean interrogation of democracy.

This return to—or of—Tocqueville occurred through a critique of regimes that claimed to base themselves on Marx: the critique of "totalitarianism." The totalitarian experience required the Tocquevillean question—that of the sovereignty of the people and the different modes of its actualization—to be posed again, but this time in an even more intense way.

Regarding "the events of '68," could one interpret them in Tocqueville's terms? The answer, I believe, is yes. Putting matters in a very condensed way, '68 was "an explosion of mildness" or "softness," an explosion of what Tocqueville called "democratic mildness." Thus, it also marked an upsurge of the democratic sentiment par excellence, that of "human resemblance." As I suggested earlier, Tocqueville saw in this sentiment the active source and intimate cause of all the transformations characterizing democratic life. And what was the most visible sign of this? The democratic eruption abolished or at least significantly diminished *distance* between the governors and the governed in the political realm (it was the end of Gaullist "hauteur") and between teachers and students in the educational realm (it was the end of "Napoleonic" discipline).

If the preceding remarks have any validity, then it is legitimate to say that the "Marxist" period of democracy, that of the social question, was preceded and followed—was in fact enveloped—by a large and powerful Tocquevillean "bed," to use a geological term. After 1968 democracy rediscovered its unchallenged authority. One could even say it attained an unprecedented degree of legitimacy. It was then that the reign of democratic consensus or uniformity began. This consensus was so powerful that communism itself, through the mouth of the Soviet leader Mikhail Gorbachev, declared itself defunct!

Do we still live in this "Tocquevillean" period? My answer, put a bit abruptly and emphatically, is no! In my view, we are now leaving the Tocquevillean period that was preoccupied with institutionalizing the sovereignty of the people and reducing social "distances" or inequalities. This period was opened in 1776 by the Americans. We can date its closure with an event that also first concerned the United States, although its consequences rather quickly revealed a growing divergence between the European and American orientations. I refer of course to September 11, 2001.

What defines this new period? Because it has barely begun I can venture only some conjectures. One important fact appears quite clearly. The sovereign state and the established people—i.e., the nation—were called into question by means of, and under the cover of, the democratic consensus at the end of the previous century. This was done in the name of democracy itself, or as a result of democracy having reached its final limits. Yet the state and the existence of an established self-governing people were the very conditions that made democracy possible in the first place.

With an unequaled comprehensiveness and precision, Tocqueville described how democracy recomposes all human relations, including the self's relationship to itself. This process of recomposition, however, took place within the context of the nation-state. Tocqueville did not seriously envisage the substantial transformation, much less the disappearance, of this particular political form. As a statesman his sole concern, his sole horizon, was "France" itself. He raised questions about the *power* or *sovereignty* of the people. Today one has to inquire about the people's very *existence*. While America recently went to war and sacrificed a good deal of its standing in world opinion for the sake of "national defense" as it understands it, Europeans find themselves in a very different situation. They are caught between their old nations and the new European Union and are perplexed as to which way to go. Europeans ask themselves: What sort of common life do we want?

Thus, we enter into a third circle, one in which the political form that is the condition of democracy is either being further developed or is on the road to being lost. The reader should imagine three concentric circles arranged on a temporal axis. The first circle is that of the social question, its diameter running from 1848 to 1968; the second circle concerns the sovereignty of the people, with its diameter joining 1776 and 2001; finally there is the third circle, that of the sovereign nation-state. Its diameter runs from approximately 1651—the year Hobbes published *Leviathan* and sketched the architectural plan of the modern state—to a date we cannot as yet give. But that date will become apparent when the nation-state gives way to another political form—if indeed that moment ever comes.

The following remarks are an effort to grasp the mainspring of the sovereign state as clearly as possible. This effort is quite urgently needed due to the differing evolution of the European nations, where this spring is ever weaker, from that of the United States, where it was recently strongly activated.

PHILIPPE RAYNAUD HAS recently underscored the following important point: the original understanding on which the modern state was founded strongly linked individual rights and public authority or power.[2] Today, however, rights have invaded every field of reflection and even every aspect of consciousness. They have broken their alliance with power and have even become its implacable enemy. From an alliance between rights and power we have moved to the demand for an empowerment of rights. The well-known phenomenon of the sovereign "power of judges" claiming to act in the name of human rights is the most visible manifestation of this trend. This elevation of rights at the expense of power—I speak here of legitimate political authority—certainly constitutes an increasingly decisive and debilitating factor at work in the political life of the European nations.

The protection, and first of all the recognition, of equal human rights was strongly tied to the construction of the sovereign state. Strongly tied—with rights serving as the moral end and the sovereign state as the political means. Put another way: the sovereign state is the necessary condition of the equality of conditions. "Sovereign" means that the state's legitimacy is qualitatively, intrinsically, unconditionally superior to any and all authorities found in society. The state is essentially superior to all social authorities, whether based on birth or wealth or on intellectual or spiritual competence. In short, the sovereign state brings equality into being; it *produces* the *plane of equality*—the equality of conditions, the equality implied in the human condition—without which we simply cannot

---

2. P. Raynaud, "Le droit, la liberté et la puissance. Portée et limites de la juridicisation de l'ordre politique," *Revue européenne des sciences sociales* 38, no. 118 (2000): 75–82.

conceive of a decent common life, despite our many differences and differences of opinion.

We must then ask why we have of late turned against this precious instrument. What animates this deep hostility toward what is, after all, conceptually and politically the necessary means to equality, the end we find most desirable? I will limit myself to three of the principal reasons.

From the conceptual and practical beginnings of the modern state it was clear that this otherwise irreplaceable instrument of our equal liberty could be turned against liberty; after all, the state retained all political legitimacy. We needed to protect ourselves against our protector. This was achieved by establishing distinctively *liberal* arrangements, whereby pride of place was given to the separation of powers. In this context, the current widespread hostility to power can be understood as a prolongation and radicalization of the "liberal" distrust, which fortunately has accompanied the modern state since its birth.

I just called the sovereign state "the instrument of our equal liberty." But one can do away with an instrument once it has done its work. One takes down the scaffolding once the building is finished. The sovereign state compelled our ancestors to acquire the mores of equality. For several generations, these democratic mores have been incorporated and assimilated. They have become our second nature, so to speak. Since we are "governed by mores"—to cite the expression Montesquieu used to characterize the Europe of his day—we no longer have any need for this outsized instrument, the sovereign state. Or so we think.

The third reason is the most relevant to us today. Contemporary democracy does not simply want to abandon this instrument, one it formerly used and found useful; nor does it want to turn away from it as though simply disgusted and ungrateful. Today democracy turns actively and aggressively *against* the state. One can generalize the comment I made earlier in reference to the democratic rejection of Gaullist "hauteur" and the reduction or effacement of distance since 1968. Democracy, as the sentiment of human resemblance, a sentiment that today grows ever more powerful and aggressive, turns against this final Difference—the superiority of the state vis-à-vis society. This final Difference, as I said, was also the first Difference, since it was the condition of equality and of human resemblance. An earlier critique of the state, put forth by conservative-minded liberals, saw the state as the instrument of democratic "leveling." We have now reached a time when the leveler is to be leveled in turn! We seem to believe that no eminence, or only of the most modest sort, should disturb the horizon, the peaceful monotony of the plains that appears to be our destiny.

The delegitimating of the sovereign state can be documented in any number of ways. The most revealing indicator is a massively significant contemporary fact that should occasion more reflection than it typically does. I have in mind the abolition of the death penalty in all European states.

I ENTER INTO the subject of the death penalty only because my broader subject demands it. To consider it requires a painful effort to think about something that disturbs all our instincts. Nor am I unaware of the history of the growing postwar movement in favor of the abolition of the death penalty. The current European consensus occurred gradually, but finally won over almost all hearts. For Europeans the abolition of the death penalty constitutes the most eloquent expression, the one dearest to their hearts, of their identity and their distinctive values. It distinguishes them from other areas of the world, including many important states in the United States that retain the death penalty. Europeans find the American retention of capital punishment almost incomprehensible. But isn't this discrepancy between Europe and the United States, on a subject upon which all democratic nations would seem to have to agree, itself derived from the great political difference between the two? That is, the United States is still a sovereign state, a genuine nation-state, whereas the European countries no longer are and no longer wish to be sovereign states, nor even nations in the full sense of the term. In any event, I will address the question *only* through this very specific political angle: the relationship of the death penalty to the principles of the sovereign state.

Let us return to the beginning, even to what preceded the beginning. Let us return to the "state of nature" as conceived by the architects of the modern state, first of all by Thomas Hobbes and John Locke. Locke underscores that, in the state of nature, each person is the *executor* of the law of nature. More precisely, this means in the state of nature, where there is no legitimate superior and no state, each individual has the right to inflict the death penalty. Of course, man in the state of nature does not have this right except in cases of legitimate defense. But under these conditions he is the sole and "sovereign" judge of what constitutes legitimate defense. Such is the original situation that must always be kept in mind.

In such a situation, where each is the judge of his legitimate defense, one arrives very quickly—one might say logically—at "the war of all against all." The state of nature necessarily ushers in a state of war, if it is not simply equivalent to it. In order to exit this state of war, which is certainly intolerable, it is necessary and sufficient that each one of us confers the exclusive right to be the executor of the law of nature on a third party. That third party now becomes the legitimate superior, and in the end he becomes the sovereign state, which is legitimate by this very act of consent. Max Weber's endlessly cited formulation—that the modern state is characterized by a "monopoly of legitimate violence"—echoes this analysis and these propositions of Hobbes and Locke.

In the state of nature, which is essentially a state of war, the death penalty is omnipresent. (It suffices for us to think of certain modern-day approximations to the state of nature: e.g., Lebanon between 1975 and 1990, certain areas of Colombia, or until recently Sierra Leone, and so on.) In the civil state the death penalty, which is now reserved to the state, has become "homeopathic"—to employ an expression of that great reader of Hobbes, Michael Oakeshott. One heals the mortal malady with a *very* small dose of the same evil. Such was the political justice of Western societies during the past three centuries.

In the past few years European countries have abolished the death penalty. Why? To repeat: I will leave aside all moral, religious, social, or properly penal considerations. I will restrict myself to the political terms of the problem as I have just presented them. The political argument against the death penalty can be formulated as follows: putting a human being to death is justified only in the case of legitimate defense. Now, this justification can hardly be valid for the state—especially the modern state, that enormous collective institution whose life is not endangered by the crimes and offenses that it must judge and punish. Consequently, the state does not have the right to put to death any member of society, no matter how criminal that person may be.

The argument is very strong. It is at the heart of the most popular moral argument against the death penalty, which states that society is not permitted to conduct itself like the criminal in putting him to death; otherwise it runs the risk of resembling him. In any case, the political argument is required for the validity of the moral argument. If we allow ourselves not to "resemble" the murderer, it is because the state is as different as is humanly possible from either the criminal or the victim, since it is invulnerable and, in Hobbes's term, "immortal." In the absence of such a state, I would be obliged to "resemble" the murderer in order to defend myself. And I would be legitimately defending myself, because we both would be in the state of nature.

As I said, the argument is strong. But perhaps it lends too much of its force to the state. I mean by this that the argument attributes to the state more power and strength than the state has or could ever have. The argument also ignores the vital moral exchange that takes place between the state and its members, the exchange that is the principle of its legitimacy and of its strength. The state requires of us not only that we do not pursue justice on our own but even that we renounce legitimate self-defense, except in very limited circumstances. Even before constraining us in this way, the state teaches us to forebear from all conduct, behavior, or even attitudes by which we *prepare* ourselves to be able to defend ourselves in the state of nature. It teaches us to lay down our natural defenses and place our confidence in the state's ability and willingness to defend us. It requires an enormous sacrifice and an immense act of faith. When a murder or a comparable crime is committed this sacrifice seems to have been made in vain and our confidence is betrayed.

For its part, the state suffers a loss of legitimacy to the extent that it shows that it lacks power. Yet today, by contrast, most Europeans think that the state which applies the death penalty both increases its weakness and loses more of its legitimacy: it "descends" to the criminal's level, thus causing all of us to fall back into the state of nature.

The argument against the death penalty can be summarized as follows: by inflicting the death penalty, the state causes us to return to the state of nature, to where it was the great instrument designed to free us. But it is precisely crimes of this sort—crimes the state could not prevent—that show that we have not completely left the state of nature. And since there will always be crimes of violent death at the hands of others we will never completely leave the state of nature behind. However, when the civil state rejects the death penalty as a matter of principle and conscience, thereby protecting the murderer of the person it could not protect, it pretends to have left the state of nature behind definitively. But by pretending this, the state severs itself from the original source of its legitimacy. And how, without extreme and shocking injustice, can the state ask me to risk my life to defend it after it has erected a new constitutional principle stating that the worst criminal will never risk his own life at the hands of the state?

IT IS IN this context we might usefully clarify the new doctrine of the Catholic Church on the death penalty. The ultimate principle of the Roman Church's teaching has not changed.[3] It resides in unreserved obedience to the divine commandment "Thou shalt not kill." That is why the church, even in the periods when it exercised its power over souls with less restraint, has always itself refused to put to death those it judged worthy of the ultimate penalty. Instead, it committed them to "the secular arm"—an exquisite procedure that managed to stir Joseph de Maistre to tears of tender admiration. Thus, the church recognized as legitimate in principle something it forbade itself from doing—putting men to death—if the one who did it was the legitimate political authority. This was one way of recognizing the validity of the political order, which otherwise was seen as a merely human thing that ruled over and for bodies. It therefore could inflict the death of the body, as the church ruled over and for souls and therefore could inflict the death of the soul. What the church bound on earth would remain bound in heaven.

Why then has the church modified, if not its very teaching on this point, at least the rules of its application?[4] Why has the church set to demanding insistently, even vehemently, that states should renounce a right that it had always recognized them to possess? Among the reasons one could advance, I believe that a reason of high politics merits particular attention.

The church cannot completely abandon its exercise of "indirect power" over the political order. Yet at the Second Vatican Council (1962–65) it accepted the principle of religious freedom. Henceforth, therefore, its exercise of its "indirect power" must

---

3. "Assuming that the guilty party's identity and responsibility have been fully determined, the traditional teaching of the Church does not exclude recourse to the death penalty, if this is the only possible way of effectively defending human lives against the unjust aggressor." *Catechism of the Catholic Church*, 2nd edition (Libreria Editrice Vaticana), art. 2267, 546.

4. "If, however, non-lethal means are sufficient to defend and protect people's safety from the aggressor, authority will limit itself to such means, as these are more in keeping with the concrete conditions of the common good and more in conformity with the dignity of the human person." Ibid.

be more and more indirect. And if the church no longer claims the right to act positively within states in the name of its divine authority, the possibility remains of doing what it can to diminish the spiritual legitimacy of these political bodies. After all, these are communities to which men have *devoted* themselves over the course of centuries, to the point of preferring the salvation of the state to the salvation of their own souls. It is therefore very coherent of the church to adopt a generally "pacifist" stance at the same time that it rejects the death penalty. It thus advances both the interior and exterior disarmament of the secular state. Should we suspect that the Church of Rome by these new teachings is only pursuing in new circumstances the old struggle between the papacy and the emperor? Be that as it may, one would have to be very insensitive to the interplay of "spiritual masses" (the phrase is Hegel's) not to detect how markedly the notion of secularization changes color— and perhaps meaning—for the church when secularization today affects political bodies as much or more as it does the church itself. Today the secular state is itself becoming secularized.

I JUST SPOKE of the papacy and the empire. In fact, its rather militant rejection of the death penalty and its rather accentuated pacifism place the church today in a profound and serious spiritual opposition to "the American empire." It is important, therefore, to consider the American attitude toward the death penalty— which as I said presents such a striking contrast to the European position. This contrast requires us to consider certain phenomena belonging to the third circle, that of the nation-state, to the extent these are unintelligible in terms of the second circle of Tocqueville's analysis. As we have seen, Tocqueville explains the progressive development of democratic "mildness" by the growing sentiment of human resemblance. Thus, there is no "democratic" reason, if I can put it that way, why the United States and Europe should find themselves at such different points on the compassion spectrum.[5] How, then, can we explain what seems to us a halt, even a regress, in democratic mildness in the birthplace of democracy, the United States? This development is even more striking when one considers that this country remains in many other respects in the avant-garde of nations when it comes to democratic sensibilities—in the relationship between the sexes, for example. Why, then, this sole exception—an exception between democratic countries and within American democratic life—when it comes to applying the death penalty? More generally, what accounts for what one could call Americans' punitive vigor and even alacrity?

In my view, it is because the Tocquevillean country par excellence has not broken with the Hobbesian scheme of the Western nation-state. There is a paradox, even a historical mystery in this, because the United States came into being by breaking with the sovereignty of Westminster.[6] In any case, the connection between the state that holds a monopoly of legitimate force and the experience of the state of nature has never completely been forgotten there. It has been maintained and even reinforced of late, even before September 11. The general recognition of the legitimacy of the death penalty goes hand-in-hand with a widespread view that each individual has the right to possess arms for self-defense.[7] Europeans believe that the Hobbesian logic

---

5. I presuppose here that abolition of the death penalty signifies a progress in "mildness" and "compassion." These two dispositions or affects, and those connected with them, would require a much more careful analysis than I can provide here. In principle, we are distrustful of our "noble feelings," but compassion seems to escape this rule of suspicion. Our compassion is revolted at the death penalty, but it seems to accept without any difficulty sufferings that occur in prison. Prison is that instrument of torment that we refuse to look at and name as such. What we really find intolerable is any *visible* assault on bodily integrity. Even in the United States one tries to reduce the visibility of this assault by means of death by lethal injection.

6. See Peter Sloterdijk: "The function of fear in politics is a problem that Americans share with Arabs: neither has really known the Hobbesian 'castration'—that is, the submission of the wild pride of the citizen to the sovereignty of the State." Peter Sloterdijk and Alain Finkielkraut, *Les Battements du monde* (Paris: Pauvert, 2003), 99.

7. This "general recognition" is far from being unanimous, I know. The past few years have seen a movement to moderate this punitive alacrity. But if democratic mildness continues to manifest itself, including at the level of the Supreme Court, it seems to

speaks in their favor, and they insist that it is contradictory to exercise a right that in principle has been yielded to the state. In turn, Americans respond that since the risk of violent death at the hands of others never completely disappears, the right to self-defense cannot completely disappear. The right to bear arms is a manifestation or component of that right. We should acknowledge that both Europeans and Americans can rightly claim to draw inspiration from the great architect of the sovereign state. But Europeans think and act as though the sovereign state has fulfilled its purpose so completely that they can now consign it to the thrift store, filed under "accessories." Americans, on the other hand, retain the feeling that they are living in a condition which makes this "accessory" necessary, even indispensable.

---

me that, above all, what is at issue in the United States is less the principle of the death penalty than the conditions of its application. I could be wrong, of course.

THE NATION

FOR MOST OF us, the destruction of the twin towers in Manhattan on September 11, 2001, did not merely represent the beginning of a series of events that would not have occurred without it and will continue into the indefinite future; it represented a catastrophe inaugurating a new epoch. To be sure, this almost unanimous sentiment very quickly gave way to lively disagreements concerning the causes and meaning of this event, as well as the characteristics of the dawning era. For myself, I cannot do better than to try to convey, if not my initial feelings, then at least what my first thoughts were after the shock of September 11.

In my view, the most deeply troubling information conveyed by the event was not its climactic revelation of terrorism as a major phenomenon. Rather, it was this: present-day humanity is marked by much more profound, much more intractable *separations* than we had thought. At a single stroke, everything we thought we knew about the dominant tendencies and the very vocation of contemporary humanity was overturned. These long term tendencies, we thought, led or even carried us irresistibly toward the unification of mankind. The fall of the Berlin Wall seemingly had placed this unification beyond doubt and even had brought it within reach. But the events of September 11, 2001, revealed the existence of another wall: the mutual impenetrability of human communities, despite the prodigious and ever-growing ease of communication.

Before that fateful day we spoke so glibly of "difference" and of "the right to difference"! This was because the "differences" we thought and spoke of could only be light and superficial, easy to combine, easy to welcome and accommodate in a reconciled humanity whose dazzling appearance would be enlivened by these differences. This was such an aesthetic vision—a tourist's view— of human things! We were suddenly recalled to political reality. Whatever their dimensions and other characteristics, human communities are dense, compact, hard to penetrate; each one is endowed with a distinctive perspective on the world. Human communities take hold of their members at a level so deep that even the powerful instruments and contagious pleasures of modern life are unable to create a truly *common* life among them.

That the majority of the terrorists came from Saudi Arabia, a close, even intimate ally of the United States; that they employed commercial airplanes, effective means of uniting human beings in a network embracing the entire planet; that they chose to destroy the most striking symbols of world commerce in the heart of the capital of the world—all these circumstances combine to confirm that the most perfected instruments of commerce and communications remain external to the lives of peoples. They are far from uniting peoples, as liberal, progressive opinion has hoped, or rather counted on, since the eighteenth century. In short, communication does not produce community.

OUR LIBERAL AND progressivist illusions concerning the powers of "communication" do have something almost irresistible to them. They find support in the oldest and most convincing definition of man as "the animal who has *logos*, articulate speech." "We are not human beings, and we do not connect with each other, except by speech," said Montaigne. How could we not expect an ever wider and faster circulation of all kinds of speech to enlarge and intensify human association? There is, however, an equivocation in this.

The bond between human association and speech is very tight, but it is not symmetrical; the two terms are not synonymous. It is not speech that produces the community, but the community that produces and maintains speech. To be sure, there are all sorts of speech and hence all sorts of communities. But all speech finds its first site and primary meaning in the political association, in the City. If human life takes place between prose and poetry, between the prose of the useful and the poetry of the noble and great, it is held together by the mediation of the just, which is the proper work of politics. The political community holds the entire register of speech together and makes it resound, and real communication is necessarily based upon this harmonic scale.

We greatly overestimate—to the point of folly—the power of the instruments of communication, and above all that of a common "vehicular" language. If we all spoke English tomorrow, we still would not have taken a single step toward unity. Israeli and Palestinian representatives, not to mention Indian and Pakistani diplomats, speak a very passable English. The instrument of a common language alone does not produce communication. Mutual comprehension presupposes that interlocutors share the same political community, or at least belong to communities whose political regimes and collective experiences are close. We Europeans also know that this necessary condition is far from sufficient. How many nations with similar regimes and historical experiences have fought each other?

We Europeans ought to be particularly sensitive to the political character of speech. European languages, we are told, are "national languages." That is true if one understands by "nation" a *political* body of a certain kind. Our languages in fact do not send us back principally to an ineffable lost origin or a series of incommunicable experiences, but to a rather intelligible political history, one to which our familiarity with the language gives access. Our languages do not express a sublime "cultural" essence that is fundamentally apolitical or metapolitical. Rather, they express the history of our respective political regimes. Take for example Racine and Shakespeare, France and England.

For each country, the poet embodies the political moment when the nation became self-conscious by attaining, as it were, its definitive form. He actualizes the potentialities of the language and at the same time "fixes," in a manner of speaking, its quantity and quality. French was the language of the court and was so firmly set in its abstract categories that it almost naturally became the language of a republic that set itself up as a schoolmaster and lecturer. It is a language of the narrative discourse that prefers the sign to the thing, a language of the tiniest and most subtle inflections. English, by contrast, had been a "barbarous" language, but one that the greatest poet of Europe very soon brought to its highest degree of expressive "ruddiness." At the same time, English was endowed with enough simplicity and force to become the very language of utility. It also is a language of imitation in which one still hears the cry of the beast, as one can regularly verify in the House of Commons. Our European languages—I have only invoked two, those best known to me—are admirable distillations brought about by that great synthesizer of European life, the nation-state.

The nation-state was to modern Europe what the city-state was to ancient Greece. It produced the unity, and therefore the framework of meaning of life by producing, in Aristotle's phrase, "the things held in common." Despite excellent historical works developing the similarities between the two, comparing the two political forms contains even more lessons that would be important to bring to light. (I have tried to do so myself in previous works.)[1] What can be said in this context is that the city-state and the nation-state are the only two political forms that have been capable of realizing, at least in their democratic phases, the intimate union of *civilization* and *liberty*. There have been great civilized empires, but even in their mildest days they lacked liberty. The life of tribes, and "primitive" existence in general, contains a very striking form of liberty; however, it does not contain the necessary conditions for establishing the amenities and charms of civilization. I would like here to consider the political form that is the nation-state, regretfully leaving aside the question of the City.

Familiarity breeds contempt. Be that as it may, we no longer know how to appreciate what the European nation-state accomplished during its historical development. It was an extraordinarily audacious endeavor, one that required mobilizing the souls not only of leaders and those who inspired them but also, of all citizens. It was an enterprise unprecedented in intensity and above all in duration, as well as in the variety of its psychic registers, as I alluded to above. The nation-state extended civic life, the condition of "living free"—which until then even in the best case had been the privilege of a small number—to associations of countless numbers of human beings. It was a matter of governing immense collectivities of men while leaving them free.

The disdain for this history has more specific and pointed causes than those of mere familiarity and habit. We are separated from our full history by the iron curtain we have erected consisting of the years 1914–45. *Before* that time, we see a thoroughly culpable history that culminated in the mud of the Éparges at Verdun and the approach-ramp at Auschwitz. *After* that time, we have come to life again, but without conversion or baptism; we wear the white

---

1. *Cours familier de philosophie politique* (Paris: Fayard, 2001), ch. 4, "La Question des Formes Politiques"; *A World Beyond Politics? A Defense of the Nation-State* (Princeton, NJ: Princeton University Press, 2006), ch. 4, "The Question of Political Forms." (Trans.)

vestment of a democracy that is finally pure, that is to say, a *non-national* democracy whose sole political program is to retain its innocence. We must step across the curtain. We must reestablish an understanding of the continuity of European history, instead of supposing that we emerged fifty years ago at the moment of the formation of the first "European" institutions after long centuries of pagan nationalism, if you will allow the expression. I would like to contribute, however summarily, to this effort.

No matter how one interprets it, one cannot but admire the long duration of the European nation-state. As conscious as one should be of the snares of historical memory, as vigilant as one should be against what Raymond Aron, quoting Henri Bergson, loved to call "the retrospective illusion of necessity," one thing is obvious: most of our nations are recognizable over the course of at least seven or eight centuries. I spoke earlier of language: who ever spoke French better than Joan of Arc before her judges? The question then arises: why this long duration, why this continuity across and despite the most enormous transformations and reversals? This is one of history's most disconcerting enigmas. Whatever reason or reasons one comes up with to account for it, one can observe that the European nations, during the course of centuries, knew how to invent new, unprecedented political instruments that would allow the adventure to continue. When the political arrangements, which were also indissolubly social and moral arrangements, seemed to have exhausted their possibilities, when they "ought to have" petrified or entered into decadence or even decomposition, Europeans knew how to invent immense and audacious artifices launched as it were like great arches over the ravines of time. Here I only will mention a few. Instead of confining themselves to a "feudalism" that would remain captive to local dominations, they constructed the strange paradox—described so well by Jean Bodin—of an absolute sovereign exercising authority over free subjects. After this arrangement exhausted its virtues with the development of the great monarchies—which were well administered and very civilized but lacked stable and regular political liberty—they instituted an equally improbable artifice: representative government.

The sovereign state and representative government are the two great artifices that have allowed us to accommodate huge masses of human beings within an order of civilization and liberty. We still live under this arrangement. However, the Thirty Years War of the previous century (1914–45) led to a profound redefinition of our political order. It is difficult to describe a process still at work. I would put matters this way: the state is less and less sovereign, and government is less and less representative. The political instruments of the democratic nation are more and more functional-bureaucratic and less and less political. Our political contrivances are more and more artificial, and each day they recede further from the natural movements of citizens' souls. What has happened?

ONE MUST FIRST note that these two components of our political arrangements are closely connected: even if the sovereign state is not necessarily representative, representative government still presupposes the sovereign state. This is true chronologically, since, as everyone knows, the latter preceded the former: Gambetta came after Richelieu![2] This is also true conceptually and politically. The point would merit a long explanation. Let it suffice to note the following: the sovereign state alone is capable of defining and simultaneously instituting the "abstract place" of representation and the plane of citizens' equality without which no democratic representation is possible. In the absence of the sovereign, the political body necessarily tends to one form or another of oligarchic domination. Therefore, there can be no representation without sovereignty.

Now, what have we seen? Or what have we done? After World War II we undertook the construction of two great artifices, one

2. Léon Gambetta (1838–82), important French politician at the time of the Franco-Prussian war, German unification, and the establishment of the Third Republic. (Trans.)

that has radically limited if not annulled sovereignty (thus at the same time affecting representation), and another that has directly changed the meaning of representation.

As for the first contrivance, I refer of course to the European construction, the "construction of Europe." It is impossible here to retrace all its stages or analyze its mechanisms. I believe, however, that it is possible to say that during the course of the fifty or so years of its development its meaning has profoundly changed. The construction of Europe began as the common enterprise of certain old European nations—primarily France and Germany—seeking to end a century of demoralizing rivalries and devastating wars and to open a viable future. That future would prolong the nations' lives but eventually (yet very much in the future) would see their convergence in a new, unprecedented political body. All this had its uncertainties and ambiguities, but it offered our exhausted nations a horizon and, as it were, breathing room, without which they would not have been restored as quickly as they were. Without Europe, there would have been no "German miracle" or "Italian miracle" or as rapid a reconstruction of France (by law in France, there can be no miracles!).

For a long time our nations and Europe developed together. But at some point, not easy to indicate exactly, but which is plausible to designate as the "Maastricht moment," the European enterprise underwent a decisive change.[3] At this point the European contrivance detached itself from the national political bodies. The artifice took on a life of its own. "Europe" crystallized as an Idea endowed with a legitimacy surpassing all others, and it was equipped and fortified with institutional mechanisms capable of reconstructing all aspects of European life. Europeans found themselves caught in an "endeavor without end," one that no longer had any political meaning. Its sole prospect was an indefinite extension that no one knew where nor how to stop. That is where we are now.

---

3. The Maastricht Treaty, signed in 1992 in Maastricht, Netherlands, went into force in 1993; by virtue of it the European Community became the European Union. (Trans.)

THE SECOND GREAT contrivance is that of the welfare state. It presents a multitude of aspects that are hard to unpack. On the one hand, it certainly represents an extension and perfection of representative government—or rather, of the representative *state*. Thanks to the welfare state, representative democracy embraced the working class, which had threatened to secede from the body politic. The working class, and more generally the "popular strata," feel themselves more "at home" in such a regime. To this extent, their desire for a change of regime—for a different regime that would truly be "theirs"—is blunted. At the same time, with the advent of this contrivance representation changes meaning, or at least loses part of its original meaning. The guarantee of "social rights" by the state, and the distribution of corresponding benefits, tended to abolish what until then had been called, in such an evocative manner, "the working-class condition." There are no longer any differences of "condition" when all citizens, in addition to enjoying equal civil and political rights, have become "rights-claimants" [*ayant-droit*] vis-à-vis the state. And the state in principle must show all an equal solicitude in connection with their "social needs." My purpose here is not to ask whether this incontestable social progress was not paid for by a certain decline in individual and even societal responsibility. The debate between "liberals" and "socialists" on this point—in American parlance, between "conservatives" and "liberals"—need not detain us here. What interests me is the paradoxical interplay inherent in representation.

The paradox I refer to presents itself approximately as follows. The vitality of the representative process presupposes that the people represented in its diverse constituent parts exists, and desires to exist, independently of representation, and thus of the representative state. In order to be represented, one must first *be*. In order to really be, one must exist in a "condition" independent of representation. The desire to be represented therefore presupposes, or contains within itself, something like the refusal to be represented—or at least a repugnance or reticence about being represented.

History verifies this. On one hand, the proletariat demanded representation at the highest levels of the nation's political institutions; but on the other, it organized its autonomy as a "class" with respect to the bourgeois state and society. It deeply distrusted the state whose recognition it demanded. One might retort that it was not always the same proletarians or workers' organizations, since some were reformist and others revolutionary. But that does not really matter, least of all from a socialist point of view. Here we are considering the representative contrivance in the inherent ambiguity of its mechanisms—that is, independently of the "subjective wills" of its various parts.

With these thoughts in mind, I would be tempted to say the following: there is no effective political representation, no genuinely vital political representation, except that acquired not only against the insufficiently representative state but also against the reluctance of each part of the people to be represented or to trust its representatives. Of course, the period I have just evoked—in France, let us say, the nineteenth and first part of the twentieth centuries—was full of social and political unrest that we take pride in finally having overcome. And to be sure, citizens during that era often found themselves furious about being "so poorly represented." But these passions gave life—often dangerous life that could not be contained by democracy—to a genuinely representative political regime.

We live under a noticeably different regime. A state whose mission consists in guaranteeing rights—not only the "liberal" rights to property and to free activity but also "social rights," or "rights as state obligations"—is being progressively substituted for the previous arrangements, which aimed at articulating and connecting the various parts of an independent people and their representatives. During a period of transition—speaking generally, after "the Thirty Glorious Years" of prosperity that followed the Second World War—citizens felt themselves rather "well represented." This was because the initial installation of the welfare state was still moved by the passions and dispositions of the earlier period. We have now moved back into a period of "representative unhappiness," this time, though, of a novel character. Citizens—the represented—agree in complaining about their representatives and more generally about the political class as a whole. The more our representatives bend every effort to show their closeness to, understanding of, and compassion for their fellow citizens, the more the latter resent and punish them.

Certainly, one important part of the dissatisfaction is due to an economic situation, or at least to economic concerns that cause anxiety. However, at the same time the total wealth of our societies continues to grow, and various indicators—starting with the health and longevity of individuals—do not suggest any decline in our "objective condition." Nor do I believe that unemployment and insecurity suffice in themselves to explain the growing alienation of the people. The loss of representative capacity in our political life is undoubtedly more important. In the case of France in particular, this loss has institutional causes, or causes relating to such political customs as "cohabitation."[4] But it seems to me that the problem is more deeply rooted. Underneath the popular anger at not being well represented one can detect anguish at no longer being representable. One can detect a fear that we are no longer a people, or at least are less and less one. This is true whether one understands this fine word "people" in the sense of a coherent "society" or in a "national" sense. Both the "societal" and the national articulations of the people have been lost or are on their way to being lost.

Ordinary language bears witness to this. There are no longer "proletarians," no longer even any distinctively "popular" elements.

---

4. "Cohabitation" is a remarkable political arrangement, the possibility of which was inherent (although unenvisaged) in the constitution of the Fifth Republic. In it a president from one political party and a prime minister from another "cohabit" or coexist. The chief architect of the constitution of the Fifth Republic, Charles de Gaulle, intended the president and prime minister to be from the same party. This, he believed, would secure unity of executive leadership. The possibility of cohabitation was first realized in 1986 with the Conservative Jacques Chirac as prime minister and the Socialist François Mitterand as president. (Trans.)

We now have only "the excluded." Thus do we designate those who, as the phrase goes, "fall through the cracks of social protection." What had been "the" people or a part of the people, what had been a rather distinctive social "condition," has now become a statistical and administrative grouping deprived of significance for the collectivity and, in the first instance, of any real meaning for the persons concerned. The poverty is the same and sometimes worse, but it is only a glitch in the social machine. Hence those pathetically vain efforts to constitute a "party of the unemployed" or "representation for the unemployed." During the course of the development of our democracy the different parts of the body politic have successively entered into the representative regime. Exclusion today refers to individuals, not to any significant part or segment. There is no longer any "social reserve" as the Marxists said, no socially independent portion, no independent "class" that could nourish an effective desire for representation. It is fine for the individual to cry out in the direction of his representatives; he will hear only the multiplied echoes of himself and his fellows ensconced in frustrating isolation.

In this way, the stage and the scene apparently remain the same and we continue to elect all sorts of representatives. But we have left the representative regime more than halfway behind. A state that universally guarantees the "human rights" of the members of society becomes a substitute for the combination of a sovereign nation-state and representative government. A state, I said. Do we need a state for that? Is it the best instrument for the job? Couldn't a regional or perhaps European administration, even a private one, do the job better? Shouldn't representative government be replaced by democratic governance?

THIS SUBSTITUTION OF "governance" for "government" in the language of politicians as well as citizens conveys the ambiguity of our dispositions toward our democracy. In fact, the term "ambiguity" is certainly too weak. We are very close to a confusion—even a contradiction—in our political sentiments.

On the one hand, we emphatically deplore both our civic apathy and the electoral revolts that regularly disturb that apathy, albeit only briefly. As for governments, they stoically observe their inability to put into practice reforms they otherwise freely declare to be indispensable, even urgent. It would be an almost irresistible epigram to say that democratic government today resembles a representative government that neither represents nor governs.

On the other hand, we warmly congratulate ourselves on the quality of our democratic *values*. Furthermore, we favorably contrast the mildness and humaneness of our mores with the vindictive moralism of American democracy—a country that, despite all our pleas, stubbornly continues to consider the death penalty an instrument of justice. When we look at ourselves in the mirror of our "values" we are rather satisfied.

How can we explain so much discouragement and perplexity on the one hand, and so much self-satisfaction on the other? Probably, what both discourages and pleases us in our collective life are two contrasting but inseparable aspects of the same phenomenon, two effects of the same cause. That cause is our political regime in the present phase of its history. Instead of increasing our ability to govern ourselves, our new instruments of government—in contrast to their predecessors, the sovereign state and representative government—shackle it more and more each day. Referring to the nations that consolidated themselves around their national currencies after the First World War, the great economic historian Karl Polanyi spoke of "a new type of nation, crustacean nations." One could say that our contemporary nations—several of which have renounced their national currencies—have increasingly thin and porous shells. But they also have prehensile instruments, by which I mean administrative instruments, that are so disproportionate and detached from the living flesh of the organisms that they have lost a great deal of their capacity to move themselves. Immobile in the increasingly precarious enjoyment of their rights, they reinterpret all human things in a way that justifies their political passivity and their spiritual inertia. Thus, contemporary European nations can be simultaneously indignant about their paralysis and self-congratulatory about their virtues, without perceiving any contradiction. Moreover, they have the ever-ready consolation of considering themselves, as parties to the European Union, to be the first instantiation, the generative association, of the growing body of a unified humanity. They count on the other members of humanity to soon join them.

This strange contemporary "depression" of the most inventive peoples in history, until recently the most capable of renewing themselves, obviously results from a great variety of factors. The rapid aging of their populations, which for some entails the not-so-distant prospect of extinction pure and simple, certainly contributes a good deal to this passivity. After all, until now the transitoriness of the individual stood in contrast to the immortality of the people. Now, while the life of the individual is extended, the life of the people shrinks to the point that the nation grows old and approaches death at least as fast as an individual does—perhaps even faster. What an extraordinary human phenomenon!

For my part, I have tried to underline the importance of the specifically political factor: the ever more paralyzing disproportion between the weakness at the heart of our political communities and the enormity of their instruments. Governed by these instruments of governance (not government), European peoples become the instruments of their instruments, the discontented but docile matter of a layering of governances. From local government to the United Nations, these governances have the sole purpose of preventing any individual or collective action that is not the simple application of a rule or regulation authorizing rights. Embracing democratic "values," we have forgotten the meaning of democracy itself—its political meaning, which is self-government, the self-government of a people. The time of enlightened despotism has returned. While this may sound harsh, it is the precise name for the sum of agencies, administrations, courts of justice, and commissions that lay down the law—or, better, rules—for us more and more meticulously. Existing in apparent disorder, all these organs are animated by the same spirit.

I HAVE JUST suggested that in the name of democracy—or more precisely, of "democratic values"—we have institutionalized the political paralysis of democracy. In the name of what is sometimes called "procedural democracy," we have emptied democracy in its original and proper sense of its substance as the self-government of a political body. A certain understanding of human action has played a great role in this development. This understanding has become increasingly narrow despite, or because, it wanted to be ever more rigorously *moral*. It is reasonable to maintain that the destruction of the properly political point of view among us has its deepest intellectual root in an ever-increasing misunderstanding of human action, of "practical life" in Aristotle's sense.

To summarize: human action no longer has any legitimacy for us, even any intelligibility, unless it can be subsumed under a universal rule of law or right or some universal "ethical" principle. The action must be able to be described as a particular application or instance of the universal rights of human beings. As I suggested earlier, this trait paradoxically connects our radical moralism to what seems to be its enemy par excellence: religious fundamentalism. For the latter, too, human action is legitimate only as the application of a Law rooted not in a shared humanity but in the sovereign will of a God who reveals that Law to a community of believers. Despite the differences in the laws to which they refer, these two conceptions make right action what is conformed to a legal rule. Thus, they make political action properly speaking very difficult. Both deprive political deliberation of any legitimacy, even of any motive or rationale. Both also render impossible—although, again, for different reasons—any elaboration of a minimal common ground between our *extreme* democracy and religious fundamentalism. Such an elaboration can be based only upon some specifically political reasoning and process. There is no general rule, no universal rule of human rights that allows us judiciously to arbitrate with some hope of arriving at mutual understanding and agreement between those who wish to affirm only "the rights of man" and those who know only "the rights of God."

LET ME GIVE an example illustrating the claim that our democratic radicalism and our "ethical" conception of human action have rendered us incapable of political action. The example that seems to me to be the most instructive for us today is the question of the admission of Turkey into the European Union and the confusion that surrounds it.

The "Turkish question" only brings to a climax a difficulty I have already discussed, a difficulty that arose from the way in which the European Union has been extended—at least after the original political proceeding was replaced by a blind process of indefinite extension. The first Europe, the "little Europe" of the six that came together in 1957, corresponded to a definite political aim that I briefly invoked above. It defined a community around a common aim. It answered the question: what to do? Once the first association was realized and showed signs of enviable success, further candidates for admission presented themselves, with different intentions and degrees of sincerity. It would have been necessary to keep a very clear focus and firm grasp on what one wanted *to do*.

General de Gaulle, it is true, denied the British candidacy; their sincerity appeared dubious to him. But how could one keep Great Britain waiting indefinitely at the door if it insisted on entering? Great Britain had so many historical claims on our admiration and gratitude. Georges Pompidou opened the door. It was done!

With that, the question changed, although we didn't know it yet. Henceforth it would no longer be: Why? It would become: Why not? And the question would no longer be posed by the founders of the association, but by the candidates for admission. No longer was it: Why do you want to enter? It would be: By what right do you leave us waiting at the door? Are we not as good Europeans as you? And in fact, the more numerous the members of the club became, the more those left outside on the sidewalk felt a very understandable anger. In the end, exhausted by a resistance that they no longer saw the sense of and that as a matter of fact no longer had any meaning, those members already in opened the door wide and everyone entered—or is about to enter. To be sure, no one is really satisfied because no one was really sincere. Each knows that the publicly celebrated result was not really willed by anyone, but rather was produced by a mechanism that no one controlled.

That, at least, is how I would briefly summarize the process that prevailed. I would add only that it was assisted and so to speak "sublimated" by the reigning moral philosophy: the idea that any legitimate or moral or just action must be "generalizable." This tends to render odious any proceeding that "distinguishes" between agents.

I come now to the subject of Turkey. The mechanism I have described contains neither a steering wheel nor a brake. It is therefore out of control. It is true that people (rather feebly) supposed that it would stop by itself, as it were, once it had reached the geographical limits of Europe. This vague idea is clearly absurd, however, since the geographical limits of Europe are only a convention, a geographical convention, we believe, without any *political* or human meaning. This is to say nothing of the absurdities entailed in eventual applications that would lead us, for example, to include Russia—but only to the Urals! Or in the case of Turkey, to include the greater part of Istanbul but not Anatolia. In addition, what motive could make *us* respect a geographic border—a mere line on a map, as we like to say—when for the past half-century we have prided ourselves on abolishing the historical and political borders that were most deeply etched in our flesh and our souls? If we can do it for the greater things, we certainly can do it for the lesser.

Thus, the "endless enterprise" of the European process encountered the lively, if not profound, desire of successive Turkish governments and probably the majority of the Turkish population. How could Turkey be refused what has been granted to so many others? Therefore, against the sentiment of the majority of their peoples and against their own instincts, the European political classes have let themselves slide toward agreeing to Turkey's admission; they are unable to conceive of any contrary, publicly presentable argument. One can hardly take seriously the ruses they have come up with in order to slow or stall things—ruses that point to Turkish deficiencies in democratic governance, which are not obviously greater than those of a good number of recent or pending members of the European Union. The effectual truth of the matter is the following: there is no doubt that the majority of European citizens and their representatives believe that the fact that populous and powerful Turkey is a massively Muslim country constitutes a major obstacle to its integration into the Union. But how can one say that?

We therefore find ourselves in an "impossible situation." But it is very clear that we ourselves have put ourselves there. This suggests that it depends upon us to extricate ourselves and finally to rediscover our *political liberty*. What is required of us is a sustained effort to relearn the elementary fact that the external acts of political bodies, including our own democratic political bodies, do not obey the same principles as domestic action. By this, I do not mean that foreign policy can disregard the ethical rules that apply to domestic action. We need to think differently—it is not simply or always a question of obeying or disobeying morality! More precisely, the requisite morality is simply that of *recognizing political reality*, which means the *objective* character of political bodies and, more generally, of human communities. "Objective": that means above all that we think independently of what we hope or fear, believe or imagine.

Within a democratic political body, within a democratic state, all citizens by definition have the same rights. These rights prohibit the political organs from discriminating among them, from treating this or that group differently—badly—because of race, religion, or their opinions. But the fact that European democracies are bound to grant their Muslim citizens a scrupulous respect for their rights—their rights *as citizens*—does not at all mean or entail that they are bound to grant a Muslim *nation* the right to take part in their community of nations. Here it is not a question of rights! By what strange confusion of thought and perversion of language could one say that Turkey, or any other country, "has the right" to enter the European councils? Perhaps it is *desirable* for one reason or another, but it cannot be a matter of right. Equal rights and equal justice have no meaning, and moreover are not possible, except among the citizens of an already existing community organized in a democratic regime.

From this standpoint, the question of Turkey's candidacy appears for what it is, not a question of moral philosophy, or an opportunity to declare our "values," but a question pertaining to what was once called "great politics." Whatever the answer might be, it ought to result from a process of widespread civic deliberation that mobilizes and synthesizes complex arguments and relates them to the essential issue.

That issue, which most Europeans grasp, I would formulate as follows: what *political form* should we give to Europe if we want her to overcome her passivity and find her place among the great agents of the present world? Properly posed, this question would lead, I believe, to excluding Turkey. Yet my purpose here is not to argue for this conclusion, but only to try to argue that it is in connection with this great issue and in these *political* terms that the "Turkish question" should be posed. Clearly, the fact that Turkey is a large Muslim country is one of the main factors—certainly not the only—that deliberation ought to take into account in a frank and sincere manner, not underhandedly, as has been the case until now. This fact would have enormous consequences for the *liberty of action* of the Union, both within and without.

But how does one conduct a political deliberation concerning a huge religious fact? What does it mean, what does it entail, to consider religion not as the indifferent matter of a universal human right within the context of a democratic order, but as a great *collective* fact, an objective political fact, one that powerfully gives form and color to our world and perhaps even determines its future? We must relearn how to speak *politically* about religion.

RELIGION

He who does not dare to steadily regard the two poles of human life,
religion and government, is a coward.
—Voltaire

HOW IS ONE to talk politically about religion? How is one to speak
objectively about it? We members of advanced European democracies
define ourselves by two ideals: the practical ideal of sincerity and
the theoretical ideal of objectivity. Hence our approach to religion:
we seek it in an interior sentiment, a subjective disposition, and we
verify it by the presence of such objective signs as participation in
worship. We suppose, for example, that a sincere Catholic regularly
attends Mass. We then measure the importance and role of the
Catholic Church in various countries by counting the number of
practicing Catholics. As Rousseau said: "Calculators, it is now your
job; count, measure, compare."[1]

"Counting," however, appears not to suffice. While some see
multiple signs of a decline, even the end of religion, others discern

---

1. J.-J. Rousseau, *The Social Contract*, bk. 3, ch. 9, in fine.

"a return to religion." I neither claim nor aim to enter into this debate, whose very terms are now contested. I want only to observe that the way the question is posed renders it even more opaque and practically insoluble. While we aspire to an objective knowledge of religion, I fear that we obey a fatal subjectivism.

For if we seek objective signs of a subjective sentiment—sincerity—we seek a will-o'-the-wisp. What could be the objective sign of a disposition that is by definition impossible to objectify? One, moreover, that great minds—Kant's for example—have denied could even be wholly sincere, because we cannot "sincerely" believe something that we acknowledge we cannot comprehend?[2] We cannot seek the objectivity of religion anywhere other than in its very objectivity. And religion is objective for us only as a *political fact*.

In any event, only in this light can I see a possible path by which to address the question that now occupies us. If it were only a question of deciding between the two positions concerning the decline or return of religion, I certainly would opt for the former, at least regarding Europe. Anyone who has seen the meager attendance of the liturgy at Saint Paul's Cathedral or the cathedral of Marseille will hesitate to speak of a "Christian Europe." But we need to leave the sanctuary and turn toward the world. We need to turn to what Montesquieu called "the present configuration of things."

How can one not see that the present world is broadly organized according to political divisions that overlap with religious ones? There is certainly something like a conflict, if not a war, between "the Christian West" and Islam. There certainly is a conflict, in truth a war—or several—connected with Israel. And is there not even an increasingly visible fracture between an "Anglo-Saxon and Protestant coalition" and another that is primarily "Catholic"? One certainly could give a nonreligious definition to each of these "spiritual masses"; for example, one could see only ruse and posturing in the "religiosity" of President Bush, or one could recall that Zionism originally was a fundamentally political and even

---

2. I. Kant, *Religion Within the Limits of Reason Alone*, bk. 4, sec. 2, no. 4.

secular movement. One could also note that today's "Islamists" have a "political agenda" as much as a religious one. And so on. In this connection, it is touching to see how observers and experts—who are for the most part nonbelievers—take such great pains to verify the religious sincerity of those they observe and study. The Inquisition was less rigorous on this point than they are!

But all this is beside the point. As I said, sincerity is among those things which are indecipherable. And even the distinction between the "political" and the "purely religious" is intrinsically unclear: politics and religion always and necessarily overlap in some measure, since both are modes of "communion." Do you think that King David was less preoccupied with politics than David Ben-Gurion or Ariel Sharon? All in all, I believe it is prudent and reasonable, even scientific, to give some credence to the world drama as it appears and unfolds before our eyes. It bespeaks *something*. True, the present configuration of things contradicts belief in "the progress of the human spirit," whether in its liberal or its socialist version. True, we counted on and placed our hopes in that belief. But let us for once believe our very own eyes.

The hesitation to admit the religious character, or coefficient, of present-day divisions often flows from a fear of aggravating them, of rendering them unmanageable by transforming them into "wars of religion." This is a commendable attitude. The American general who publicly declared that "we are at war with Islam, itself an evil religion," merited the condemnation he received. However, our obligation to act in a responsible manner that does not inflame passions does not diminish our other obligation, that of trying to understand the world. And if perchance it were true that "we are at war with Islam," it would be of paramount importance to know this, not only in order to win the war—since I imagine that we would not want to lose it—but also to prepare seriously the peace. I do not believe that we are at war with Islam, but I try to be in a position, or disposition, that would not prevent me from recognizing it if such were the case.

IF WE ARE not at war with Islam, it is important to avoid talk of a "war of civilizations." First of all, civilizations do not make war. This sad privilege is reserved to political bodies. Now, the political problem of Islam is precisely that it has not found its proper political form. In saying this, I make no special claim about Islam, since I have no credentials in that regard. I only want to draw attention to some well-known facts.

A number of Europeans or Westerners moved by benevolence counsel Islam to reform itself—that is, to undertake a number of religious, social, and political reforms that will allow Muslims finally to participate fully in the emerging, common world of a united humanity. This sort of advice comes naturally to us because Europe has a particularly long and rich experience of such profound changes, in which the human association that changes nonetheless preserves its subjective continuity. I earlier indicated that this was a special virtue of the "time of nations." The "nationalization" of Christianity by the Protestant Reformation both sheltered Christianity and entailed its "subjectivization." Hegel wrote: "Luther would not have accomplished his Reform if he had not translated the Bible into German." The ability to welcome change and the desire for subjective appropriation of the various "contents of life," including religious contents, depend upon each other. This desire finds support in the confidence we have in our ability to persist in our subjective or personal identity through the changes of life. Is this combination exclusive to "Christian Europe"?

In the interpretation it gives of itself, Islam closes the monotheistic revelations with the definitive revelation, a divine Law received and transmitted by Mohammed. The divine Law is immediately positive and manifestly rational. Obedience to it constitutes the *umma*, "the supreme community," a community of equals in which there is no "spiritual authority" as in Christianity. There are only imams who lead prayer and jurists who interpret the divine Law; but these are not theologians. To this distinction, one could add that Islam lacks the distinction found in the Christian world between the visible and the invisible church, and thus any tension between the institutional and spiritual poles. In a manner of speaking, Islam is located entirely in its external, objective characteristics. This absence of interior divisions—between temporal and spiritual, visible and invisible—is obviously a great principle of strength. The relationship of Islam to territory is another principle of force and "objectivity" in that every conquered land where the divine Law is applied becomes Islamic; it becomes part of the "house of Islam," a "house" which normally includes geographical continuity. Outside this "house of submission" is "the house of war," where *jihad* is legitimate and, depending on the circumstances, even required.

These very summary statements are enough for my purpose. If we seek to characterize Islam as a human association—or as I prefer to say, as a political form—we would probably say that it is an empire, or at least that it belongs to the genus of empire. While very important despite its apparent simplicity, this conclusion does not adequately define the political nature of Islam. But can that nature be completely defined? If one can recognize the form or at least the imprint of empire in Islam, one must still say that no one political regime characterizes Islam. The closest thing to it is found in Sunni Islam, the majority form of Islam, in the so-called Medina utopia—the perfect political order realized in Medina from 622 to 632 A.D., when the Prophet was legislator, head of the city, and war leader. But this is an inimitable model, even if it can fuel the imagination. In practice, power was vested in the caliph. Coming in principle from the Prophet's tribe, his task was to preserve the religious foundation of society, that is, *sharia*. Normally, the caliph has recourse to consultation and he aims at unanimity. But the caliphate is only a political formula—the term "regime" does not really apply—and it is so underdetermined that Islamic political life historically experienced a particularly stark division between legitimacy and necessity. While waiting for the impossible realization of the perfect model, one usually accommodated oneself to a political life very far removed from the Law. One can see in this fact one of the main causes of the difficulty Islam has had in effectively practicing democracy. On one hand, the unquestionable Law excludes or severely limits many of the personal liberties that democracy requires; on the other, the enormous latitude of conduct enjoyed by princes or leaders is incompatible with respect for democratic laws. Here is a debilitating chiasma from which Islam has great difficulty extricating itself.

Returning to our initial thoughts, the political form closest to Islam is the empire; its last instantiation was the Ottoman empire. Until 1924, Muslims thought there were successors to the Prophet. But Mustafa Kemal abolished the caliphate on March 3, 1924, and from then on Islam has been an empire without an emperor.

The empire is a typical form of ancient politics. One could say that in political terms "to modernize" is to find an alternative to empire. The Europeans' political development was characterized by their simultaneous effort both to govern themselves and to attain self-awareness by escaping from a double imperial matrix: from the Roman empire on one hand and the Catholic Church on the other—specifically, the *Roman* Catholic Church, because it assumed the imperial form. At the end of a lengthy process, one had "Christian nations," which meant that the political form had changed from empire to nation, as had the religious form, since the substantive had become an adjective. To explore the full meaning, much less evaluate the merits, of this immense transformation is totally beyond my aim in this work. I invoke it simply to note that Islam has not experienced such a transformation, or an analogous one. Hence the political infertility of the tardy national or nationalist movements in Muslim countries; here, recourse to the idea of the "Arab nation" only designated precisely *what was lacking*.

We therefore find ourselves in the presence of an immense empire, or at least an immense imperial imprint, without an emperor. It is an immense sensitive surface—how very sensitive indeed!—having no coherent internal articulation. As a result, the Arab Muslim world is subject to various waves of this or that kind of mobilization. Be they "national" or "fundamentalist," these waves really reveal the form that is lacking, that fails to be actualized, whether the nation or the empire. The Arab Muslim world thus displays enormous strength in terms of numbers and extension due to the stability and objectivity of its religion, and enormous weakness due to the absence of an effective political form. For only such a form would allow it to make new appropriations—at once faithful and transformative—of the Prophet's teachings.

We thus confront and present a contrast to what one might call the stark objectivity of Islam and the slide into subjectivity of the West. Both sides seek or need what is lacking: their contrary, their complement. Islam has thus far sought in vain a subjective appropriation that could make it the religion of free men and women, while the European nations of today have also thus far sought in vain an objective definition of themselves. If they have tried to form a site for merely transitory encounters of their free subjects, they have run up against the objectivity of Islam. If Islam is our enemy, it is in the sense in which Theodor Däuber, in a very striking formulation, wrote: "The enemy is the figure of our own question."

WHEN "ISLAMISTS" DESIGNATE Europeans or Americans as "crusaders," we tend to shrug our shoulders before this indication of their sad inability to liberate themselves from "historical traumas." We certainly do not think of ourselves as crusaders! And we emphatically do not think that we are Christians. Or when we are, it is under the rubric of the exercise of our subjective freedom, as a choice that we can always revisit. "To be a Christian" is for us simply a possible decision. What we really are is inscribed in our political regime, whose pivot is the "neutral" or "lay" state that guarantees equal rights—especially freedom of conscience—to everyone, believer and nonbeliever alike. We therefore do not recognize ourselves at all in the mirror held up to us by the Islamists. But does our "neutral and agnostic state" really suffice to define us?

We French are especially inclined to overestimate the powers of the secular state. In doing so we remain not only prisoners of a particular history but imprisoned in a particularly narrow understanding of that history. We forget that the establishment of the secular state presupposed the prior establishment of a new sacred community, the nation. The state could not become neutral unless the French nation previously had become (at least for the vast majority) "the community par excellence," thus superseding the church. For the secular state to become possible, it was necessary for "very Catholic France" to become simply "France." It was necessary for the affirmation "I am French" to contain the meaning of unreserved devotion to the French nation and people.

As soon as this understanding and feeling for the nation have been lost or deliberately abandoned, the secular state cannot maintain itself, or can do so only for a little while. Even this requires theatrical demonstrations that are less and less genuine and more and more unpleasant. The "republican" uproar that accompanied the prohibition on Islamic headscarves is a good example and harbinger. The secular state cannot survive the nation. Its neutrality depends upon its "transcendence," and its transcendence derives from the fact that it is the instrument, the "secular arm," of the nation. Once the nation is abandoned as a sacred community, the lay state itself is laicized and becomes merely one of the innumerable instruments of governance I described above. The communities that until now were subordinate to the nation detach themselves from it and aspire to self-sufficiency.

THE MOST REVEALING sign of this transformation has not been the "difficulties of integration" experienced by the Muslim community. After all, the Muslims are relative newcomers. Rather, it has been the troubles and perplexity that have gripped the French Jewish community, or at least a significant number of its members. This community is profoundly and intimately a part of the history of modern France, and its contributions to the life of the nation are as great as ever. Today, however, it experiences anxiety over an unprecedented *separation*. This separation, moreover, is desired rather than suffered, or at least is desired at the same time it is experienced. In any case, unprecedented tensions make themselves felt. We can shed light on these by recalling the classical Republican arrangements, or rather, the original Republican intention.

In his "testament" of March 18, 1941, the French historian Marc Bloch wrote the following:

> A stranger to all confessional formalism, as well as to all purportedly racial solidarity, all my life I have felt myself, above all and quite simply, to be a French-man. I am attached to my country by a long family tradition, I have been nourished by its spiritual legacy and its history: I am in truth incapable of imagining another country where I could breathe at my ease. I have already much loved and served her with all my strength. I have never found that my identity as a Jew placed the smallest obstacle to these sentiments. During the past two wars it was not my fate to die for France. I can say in all sincerity, though, that I die, as I lived, as a good Frenchman.[3]

I hesitate to bring such a marvelous text into an argument or to treat it as a "document." At the same time, such a text enables us to take the measure of the extent of the change that has affected French Jews' relationships with both the history of the Jewish people and with France.

The way one writes history and judges its protagonists depends on "the community of reference," "the community par excellence," in whose light one proceeds. In saying this I do not speak of freeing

---

3. Marc Bloch, *L'Étrange Défaite* (Paris: Gallimard, 1990), 212. Originally published in 1946. (English language edition: *Strange Defeat* [Norton: W. W. Norton & Co., 1999].) (Trans.)

oneself from national or ethnic prejudices in order to render an impartial judgment. I presuppose our good will, our scruples, and our impartiality. Rather, I ask whether the "horizons of meaning" of the various communities of reference overlap and form a "common framework" within which one can finally discern the truth of history. If that common framework exists, can human beings come to know it? For example, concerning the theological-political conflicts that structured and punctuated the history of Europe, how can one attain a higher plane from which to view and judge the totality of actions of both those who belonged to the "profane" political body, the nation, and those who adhered to the church or churches?

In the particular case of the Jews, the moral and political landscape dramatically changes for a French Jew depending on whether he considers himself first and foremost a member of the "French people" or first and foremost a member of the "Jewish people."[4] The two affiliations certainly are not mutually exclusive, and each French Jew combines them in a manner all his own, a manner that gives a particular stamp to his character as a citizen. At the same time, while the connections can vary over the course of a lifetime, a certain law requires that one be deeper and stronger than the other. Of course, some will retort: Who are you to probe these matters, you who can only consider them from the outside? I admit that I must appear quite intrusive and ham-handed to those who feel the complexity of these things within themselves.

---

4. The "testament" I cited in footnote 3 above shows that Marc Bloch considered himself first and foremost a member of the French people. In the text of a petition he wrote to the president of the General Union of the Jews of France in the name of "French Jews"—dated February 9, 1942—one can even read the following: "Whatever might be the differences of our philosophical, political, or religious convictions, we belong to the French people, it is ours. We know no other." Ibid., 314. We must add, however, that the word "people" does not bear the exact same meaning in each case. Belonging to the Jewish people means something different from belonging to the French or English or American people. For a Frenchman, an Englishman, an American, belonging to the people necessarily implies being a citizen of a national polity. Belonging to the Jewish people occurs independently of all political contexts, including the national one. This led Raymond Aron to write: "If there is a Jewish people, no other people of the same type exists." See Aron's *Mémoires* (Paris: Julliard, 1983), 505.

We can escape from the paralyzing uncertainties of subjective interpretation if we take the time to consider the major political fact of the modern history of the Jewish people: Zionism. With the Zionist movement, Israel broke out of the protective "hedge of the Torah" and attempted to become a "nation like the others," and the Jewish people a people "like the others." With the Zionist movement, Israel itself aimed to join or even produce the "common framework" I spoke of earlier, one in which it hoped to encounter the other nations in mutual equality and recognition. To be sure, rabbinical Orthodoxy condemned the Zionist movement insofar as it implied "the violation of the vows taken by Jews at the time of the diaspora."[5] But it is undoubtedly true that the formation of Israel profoundly changed the condition of *all* Jews, whatever their relationship to the Jewish tradition.

It is important to underscore that Zionism was a national movement that emerged from the nineteenth century, the century of national movements in Europe. One could even say that Zionism marked a synthesis of all the "-isms" produced by the nineteenth century: not only liberalism and nationalism but also socialism and syndicalism. Is Israel not the only state that one can say was originally founded, or at least originally governed, by a movement that combined socialism, syndicalism, and nationalism? In this light one might say that Zionism would not have succeeded if the Second World War and destruction of the Jews of Europe had not profoundly changed the political, moral, and even emotional conditions of the Zionist enterprise. But one must recall that Zionism was not originally directed against Hitler's murderous hatred. It first confronted the good intentions of liberalism.

In their founding affirmations, Leon Pinsker and Theodor

---

5. Alain Dieckhoff, *L'Invention d'une nation. Israël et la modernité politique* (Paris: Gallimard, 1993), 170. The "oaths" are the following: "not to live in Eretz Israel in large numbers or by force of arms (as long, that is, as the Messianic era has not begun) and not to rebel against the nations of the world" (ibid.).

Herzl "started from the failure of the liberal solution."[6] Leo Strauss formulated the problem in these terms:

> Liberalism stands or falls by the distinction between state and society, or by the recognition of a private sphere, protected by the law but impervious to the law, with the understanding that, above all, religion as particular religion belongs to the private sphere. Just as certainly as the liberal state will not "discriminate" against its Jewish citizens, so is it constitutionally unable and even unwilling to prevent "discrimination" against Jews by individuals or groups. To recognize a private sphere in the sense indicated means to permit private "discrimination," to protect it and thus in fact to foster it. The liberal state cannot provide a solution to the Jewish problem, for such a solution would require a legal prohibition against every kind of "discrimination," i.e., the abolition of the private sphere, the denial of the difference between state and society, the destruction of the liberal state.[7]

As soon as it became apparent that Jews could not recover their full dignity by individual "assimilation" in the national societies to which they belonged, they were forced—forced by self-respect and necessity—to found a national society in which "discrimination" would be impossible: in other words, a Jewish state.

The way Strauss describes the structural impossibility of a liberal solution to "the Jewish problem" through "assimilation" shocks us in its brutality. It leaves us with no hope. We therefore are tempted to reply that Strauss inappropriately generalized a particular historical situation, the one in which Zionism was originally formed. And, we add, the liberal France of today has

---

6. Leo Strauss, *Spinoza's Critique of Religion*, preface to the English translation (New York: Schocken Books, 1965), 4.

7. Ibid., 6.

next to nothing in common with the liberal France of the time of the Dreyfus Affair. Today, neither the state nor society would allow anti-Semitic discrimination among us, whether against individuals or groups.

This retort has its validity, but it underestimates two important connected points. The first is suggested by the Straussian analysis itself. The effort to outlaw and stamp out any and all discrimination in society would lead, he said, to the destruction of the liberal state. We are not at that point yet, but it is clear that the struggle against "all forms of discrimination" has caused us to depart from the original liberal regime. We live under a "disciplinary regime" of what is called "political correctness," which forbids us to consider one another under any rubric or category besides "the similar." What *distinguishes* or differentiates us cannot be evaluated or even publicly named. Like others, Jews are protected by this discipline.

The second point, tied to the first, involves public awareness of what had been inflicted upon the Jews of Europe. Such awareness could occur only gradually, since the Holocaust so tremendously dwarfed the human imagination. Eventually, though, it bestowed a sort of particular protection in public opinion on Jews. But these circumstances do not belong to the liberal regime as such; thus, no one knows how long their effects will be felt. As a matter of fact, one feels them weakening already.

It is therefore understandable why, in Strauss's eyes, Zionism was the morally necessary response—Strauss does not say, the fully satisfying response—to the failure of the liberal solution to "the Jewish problem." The failure of the liberal solution means that Jews cannot recover their honor as Jews by becoming individual citizens "like the others." But can they form a nation "like the others"? This was the conviction and hope of *political* Zionism, the Zionism of Pinsker and Herzl. These two shared the confidence of the century of "nationalities" in the capacity of peoples for self-determination.[8] The most striking indication of the political character of their faith

---

8. The title of Pinsker's manifesto is *Auto-Emancipation* (1882).

is that, in the beginning at least, they did not believe it necessary to establish the Jewish state on the land of Israel.[9] But if the state could be separated from the land, then it could also be separated from any and all properly Jewish traits, starting with the Jewish religion. Following this logic to its end, what would ultimately distinguish "the Jewish state" political Zionism proposed? What would distinguish it from a non-Jewish liberal state wherein Jews would be "assimilated," where no "discrimination," even private discrimination, would be possible? The gain would be minimal if its citizens led a life that had "nothing Jewish" about it.

As we all know, an irresistible gravitational force led Jews to the Promised Land, and the construction of the Jewish state occurred during a series of "returns."[10] People wanted to believe that a "people without a land" returned to a "land without a people," one that belonged to it pure and simple. In this connection Ze'ev Jabotinsky, the "father of the Zionist Right," made an argument that is worthy of consideration. His argument reconciled an affirmation of the absolute justice of the Zionist cause with recognition of the presence of Arabs in the land. In February 1937, appearing before the Peel Commission charged with investigating the Great Arab Revolt that had broken out the year before, Jabotinsky said that "to compare the Arab claim with the Jewish claim in terms of their safety and security is to compare plenty with famine."[11] Not only was the very existence of the Jewish people threatened, but as Alain Dieckhoff puts it,

> the Arab inhabitants of Palestine could not be severed from the wider Arab people: the national question is properly posed not between Jews who reside in Pal-estine and Palestinian Arabs, but between Jews the

---

9. In 1903, Herzl agreed with Joseph Chamberlain's proposal to grant Jews the land of Uganda. He soon abandoned the idea, though.

10. Normally five are counted, starting with the *aliya* that occurred contemporaneously with the first Russian pogroms and continuing to the results of the Nazis' policies.

11. Quoted in Alain Dieckhoff, *L'Invention d'une nation*, op. cit., 214.

world over and Arabs as a whole. At the global level, justice requires that a wandering, scattered, country-less people should obtain from the Arab people—who are spread throughout enormous lands—and from the international community a parcel of land, land in the Middle East where it was born as an historical entity.[12]

Jabotinsky's argument is quite relevant to our reflections, in addition to its intrinsic political interest. Recognizing that the Arab world lacked a national form, he concluded that the Arabs of Palestine could not claim self-determination, which presupposes the existence of this form. We have already seen how important the question of political forms is for understanding the relations between Christians and Muslims. We are not surprised, then, that it is also relevant to understanding relations between Jews and Arabs. What Jabotinsky's argument lacks, however, is awareness of the political dynamic introduced by the establishment of a Jewish nation in Palestine—the almost irresistible appeal that this national "edification" had for the Palestinians. By displaying the example and model of a desirable national life, Israel stimulated Palestinians to desire such a life for themselves. Palestinians thereby became among all Arabs perhaps the most capable, because the most desirous, of such a life. Are these desires superficial movements of Palestinian subjectivity that are destined to be absorbed in and by the insurmountable objectivity of Islam? That could be. But in the interim, one cannot halt the "contagion" of the principle of self-determination, a "subjective" principle that belongs to anyone who adopts it.

If the Palestinians rather quickly turned the power of this subjective principle against Israel, Jews themselves experienced its limits, if not its weakness. I said earlier that, as free in its choices as political Zionism thought itself to be, it finally had to yield to the attraction of the Promised Land. The self-determination of

12. Ibid.

Jews could do nothing against the objectivity of the past and the fecundity of the Jewish religion. True, the state of Israel today hardly resembles the Jewish state envisioned by Herzl. Nonetheless, the relationship of contemporary Jews with, even their dependence upon, the original religious definition of Israel has not been abolished. This is true even if the great majority of Jews, whether in Israel or in the diaspora, have abandoned the traditional form of Jewish life and consciousness in favor of a "modern," liberal understanding of their lives as individuals and citizens. Whatever their subjective dispositions—and from time to time these include a lack of sympathy for Israel—every Jew today lives in a situation determined by the existence of a Jewish state. And this state, with its leaders and citizens who are often preciously little "religious," and sometimes very hostile to the demands and "privileges" of the orthodox, cannot break—indeed, it does not *want* to break— entirely with the Jewish Law or Torah. If it did, it would cast Judaism as mere "folklore" and thus destroy it.

The list of paradoxes presented by the state of Israel is long. Among them, we can note the following. The effort at Jewish self-determination, the effort to gather together into a nation "like the others," only gave new form to Israel's distinctive, even singular, destiny—to its "election." The elders of Israel went to Ramah to ask Samuel "to appoint for us a king to govern us like all the nations."[13] However, elsewhere we read: "What is in your mind shall never happen—the thought, 'let us be like the nations.' . . ."[14]

WHAT WE ARE inclined to underestimate are the effects the establishment of the state of Israel had on "the European condition." First of all, that state was the product of an "exodus from Europe." But Europe was slow to take the measure of the depth of the repercussions she herself felt. After the war, the European nations that were democratically rebuilding looked sympathetically on the

---

13. 1 Samuel 8:5.
14. Ezekiel 20:32.

construction of the Jewish democracy. Generally speaking, their governments shared a sentiment that was clearly more positive than those expressed at the time by the United States. This is often forgotten today. This European sympathy was especially strong among British and French socialists, who exhibited a particular admiration for David Ben-Gurion. But this disposition culminated, and ended, on the occasion of the Six-Day War. General de Gaulle's press conference of November 1967 marvelously expresses the transition. It displayed the principle motive and inner dynamic of a rupture that was experienced as such and caused equal parts dismay and misunderstanding on both sides. It shocked Raymond Aron, who wrote his famous pamphlet *De Gaulle, Israël et les Juifs* in response.[15]

De Gaulle's discourse, even his voice, expressed the rupture perfectly. Its broken cadence, and the marked alteration of his tone of voice, help us see and measure the changes that the Israeli victory—Israel's conquests—both effected and provoked. *Before* was the establishment of the Jews in their own state and in the Promised Land. This was accompanied by hosannas of widespread approval and, "above all, one must say, in Christendom," combined with "pity" for "ancient misfortunes" and recent "abominable persecutions." To both were joined "sympathy" or fellow feeling for "their works of construction and the courage of their soldiers." *After* . . . "After" had just barely begun. But the earlier events of 1956 had already revealed "a bellicose state of Israel," one "resolved to expand."

In 1956, however, Israel had not attacked without previous consultation and coordination with Great Britain and France. In 1967 it attacked, despite the most insistent urging of General de Gaulle not to do so. It thereby "escaped" from Europe, breaking

---

15. This text can be found in *Essais sur la condition juive contemporaine*, assembled and annotated by Perrine Simon-Nahum (Paris: Éditions de Fallois, 1989). General de Gaulle's press conference is reproduced on pages 37–40 of that volume. English language edition: Raymond Aron, *De Gaulle, Israel, and the Jews* (New Brunswick, NJ: Transaction Publishers, 2002). (Trans.)

with many Europeans and their sympathy, a sympathy that had both enveloped it and held it in check. At this point, I should perhaps reaffirm that my purpose in recalling these events is not to judge the Israeli action, or for that matter de Gaulle's attitude. It is rather to capture the political moment when Israel declared, as it were, its full spiritual independence and when General de Gaulle expressed the chagrin and resentment of old Europe.[16]

As well "assimilated" as Jews might be in the various European countries, after 1967 these countries had increasing difficulty in understanding the meaning of the political and spiritual "whole" that the Jews and Israel henceforth constituted. Thus, they had more and more difficulty in sympathizing with Israel. They could no longer relate to Israel simply as a fellow democracy, or even as the only democracy in the Middle East, no matter how true these claims. A distance was created, and a certain doubt took root.

From the "maternal" embrace of France (a phrase Marc Bloch still invoked, ironically at the very moment of the cruelest abandonment) Israel succeeded in gaining total emancipation.[17] Soon enough, as the Jews assumed all their prerogatives as a people and managed—with legitimate joy and pride—all their internal affairs, the European peoples took stock of their weaknesses and confessed their crimes. They seemed to want to disappear, to blend into the general humanity that had earlier embraced the Jews. But now, Israelis appeared to prefer their particular existence. What an inexplicable reversal! Do these ironic and painful reversals have any meaning?

Israel's establishment poses a much more difficult, at least a more "intimate," question to European nations than the one posed by the arrival—or return—of Islam. European democracy today

---

16. General de Gaulle concluded his recitation of the French efforts to avoid war, in particular his conversation with the foreign minister Abba Eban, with the following words: "One sees that France's voice was not heard."

17. "At the same title as our Catholic or Protestant compatriots, among whom we count so many dear friends and fellow former combatants, we believe ourselves to be loyal and grateful sons of this common mother" (see Bloch's petition to the president of the UGIF in *L'Étrange Défaite*, 314).

can see virtue only in what is "general" or "universal." But the Jews testified to the limits first of Christianity and then of the liberal nation-state. And while their destiny seemed to call for the advent of a unified humanity, one not broken by any internal division or separation, they could build Israel only with a constant, even daily struggle; today, this struggle calls for the construction of a long fence. For Europeans, the Jewish state thus displays the limits of a universalism they believed to have deduced, in part, from the longtime misfortunes of the Jews. That state obliges Europeans to recognize the following: empty—hollow and vain—is any humanism that claims to detach itself wholly from all responsibility toward or for a particular people, or from any distinctive view of the human good. Empty and vain is a Europe that wants simply to meld into the growing body of "humanity in general." The fully national existence of little Israel questions enormous Europe, as well as each nation that composes it. It invites them not to hide behind Humanity.

HOW DO EUROPEANS respond? What do we answer? We oscillate between two responses that reduce to one. I just alluded to the first, which is only a refusal to answer. Since we believe that the European Union is the avant-garde of Humanity in the process of its definitive unification, we have no other point of view than that of Humanity itself. According to the second answer, we do have a distinctive "European point of view"—one that means, especially, "not American." More positively, that view derives from "European culture" and is founded on "European values." And what are these "European values"? The European value that comprehends all the others is "openness to the Other," a universalism "without any borders or limits." European particularism thus resides in a particularly generous openness to human generality or universality. Whatever one might think of this generous interpretation of our generosity, one has to recognize that we refer to "Europe" only in order to cancel it. We only know Humanity! We do not possess any particular existence; we do not want to possess in any shape, manner, or form a distinctive existence of our own, one that would necessarily be particular.

Let us grant for the sake of argument the European claim to be a pure absence, even in the midst of various surrounding presences: the Chinese, the Americans, the Israelis. Let us admit that we signify something when we speak of "European values." If we are so "open to the Other," we should undoubtedly be open to what the Other says about us. We should take it seriously and evaluate it with conscientious care. We have seen that neither Muslims nor Israel identifies Europe with Humanity itself. They find us more "substantial" than we find ourselves! In fact, they sometimes find us rather "dense."

Since it is others who say these things, it is likely that despite our protestations we are something in *particular*.

We do not need to look very far to find this something in particular. We are not in search of an unheard-of name or sophisticated definition here! Above all, let us not seek our particularity in the future—in a new regime, in a "new man." We have already tried that. Most recently, we have made a show of having discovered or invented a truly new form, and we have contained ourselves in a single word, "Europe." Now, however, we are in the process of leaving even that behind, having discovered that the word contains nothing; or rather, that this word conveys something else—another thing. I shall explain.

As Freud famously said, truth is often conveyed by a slip of the tongue. The effort to define Europe, or rather *not* to define it, has been the occasion for an enormous collective slip of the tongue. "Europe is not a Christian club," went the mantra. I do not know where it originated, but it was picked up and repeated by all the authorized voices. Analysis of this proposition is neither easy nor simple.

First of all, it is clear that the European Union originally was a club, that the founding members both conducted themselves and admitted others as members of a club—even if, as we saw earlier, they were finally inundated and submerged by new "members." Next, there never has been and cannot be a "Christian *club*": new members of the church are not voted in but received into *communion*. If the European Union originally was a club, and if there can be no Christian club, what does it mean when one says that Europe is not a Christian club? It means, of course, that Europe is not Christian—but one cannot say that. Something inhibits us from saying that Europe is not Christian. The only thing inhibiting us from saying this is that Europe is in fact Christian.

Here one must pay close attention. The affirmation does not mean "that Europeans are Christians." Such an affirmation pertains to data and statistics and would require an objective knowledge of subjective sentiments—something that I suggested at the beginning of this chapter is impossible to determine. And if we content ourselves with likelihoods, the affirmation is hardly likely, as I also said earlier. Nor does it pertain to the category of "the desirable." It contains no implicit or explicit appeal to a future re-Christianization of Europe. Here I am not interested in transforming the world, only in understanding it. And understanding the Christian character of Europe is something that is open to the nonbeliever as well as the believer. Finally, I am not making any claim concerning "culture," as when someone affirms that we are still "a Christian culture." In saying that, I believe that one is uttering nonsense, or—more charitably—that one is confusedly pointing to what I am trying to highlight, something objective and political.

I am not looking for subjective sentiments but for the political articulations of the common world. By "constructing Europe," by "enlarging the European Union," we have tried once again to leave Europe and our European condition behind. Once again, and perhaps for the last time: after the sacred nation, after class, after race, we try to escape from the European condition in the name of "Europe" itself. Our leaders, our governors, certainly are doing this. But they encounter resistance. They can shout themselves hoarse and lecture us on our hesitancy, our recalcitrance, but it seems that this time, too, the effort will be in vain. Our condition as Europeans is stronger than even our strongest passions. It is in the process of recapturing us.

In returning to Israel, the Jewish people achieved its "exodus from Europe." By this I mean that thanks to the establishment (or reestablishment) of its own state, it ceased to be spiritually dependent upon the European nations within which it lived and still lives. This was the result, the culmination, of a long historical sequence. It resulted not only from the destruction of European Jewry but also from the self-effacement to which European nations have devoted themselves for the past twenty years with an enthusiasm that simply astonishes. Having thus "departed from Europe," the Jewish people invite Europe to utter its own name. They ask Europe its name.

Europe, however, attempts to escape from this obligation, "responding" by hiding itself in the crowd and transforming itself into a crowd. Its "members" are never enough! It thereby seeks to postpone indefinitely an answer to the question of what "body" it constitutes or to which it belongs. But the spiritual vacuity of a Europe of "indefinite extension" is such that this question returns with heightened urgency. Who can live in a human world devoid of any form?

LET US, THEREFORE, return to and "reenter" the real Europe that we are trying vainly to leave. Let us rediscover familiar territory. The promise of communion that was contained in the Christian message and first deployed in the Roman Church and the Christian empire was adopted and refracted into the language and mores of each nation in order that it might be appropriated more deeply. The Christian nations went so far as to absorb the church, even to the point of transforming the nation into a church. The democratic idea marked at once a repetition and a simplification of the promise of communion. It sparked the actualization of the powers and potentials of the nation.

Why, though, should the weakening of the European nation today—and its further humiliation beneath rules and regulations—mean the end of the political form of the nation-state? In truth, we have no other form. But we should not confuse the nation with the church. This painfully acquired wisdom returns to the foreground that even larger European communion which we hesitate to acknowledge or name. It is a happy hesitation in one sense: I do not advocate putting the Christian name on battle standards! Preserving the nation is rather a question of continuing the European adventure. And this means continuing its current phase, one, after all, that has sought to connect liberty and communion as closely as possible, to the point where the two become as one.

APPENDIX A:
DEMOCRACY WITHOUT NATIONS?

IF WE TRY to characterize the late-twentieth-century political world, our first observation would no doubt focus on the victory of democracy, with 1945 and 1989 marking the dates of the collapse (in quite different ways) of the two most terrible enemies that democracy faced in the twentieth century.[1] This does not mean that democracy is everywhere peacefully established, nor that where it *is* established it may not encounter considerable difficulties. It means, rather, that the democratic principle of legitimacy no longer has a politically credible rival anywhere in the world. Even the upheavals associated with "Islamic fundamentalism" do not, in my view, undermine the general validity of this appraisal. Be that as it may, I will consider here only the Western world.

---

1. This essay originally appeared in the Fall 1996 issue of *Commentaire*. It first appeared in English in *Journal of Democracy* 8:2 (1997), 97–102. © National Endowment for Democracy and the Johns Hopkins University Press. Reprinted with permission of the Johns Hopkins University Press.

The democratic principle of legitimacy is the principle of *consent*: a law or obligation is not legitimate, nor am I bound to obey it or fulfill it, unless I previously have consented to this law or obligation through myself or my representatives. A democratic regime, therefore, is that regime which in principle is willed by each individual. This is because a democracy defines itself as, and seeks to be, that regime which is willed by each individual. With this starting point in mind, how could anyone want anything but democracy? It is quite striking to observe that even during the period of their greatest strength, totalitarian regimes officially deferred to the principle of consent by organizing elections. This is also what the Islamic Republic of Iran does today. In other words, once the principle of consent has been brought to light, even its most resolute adversaries spare no effort in extorting from their populations formal signs of the most unanimous possible consent.

In a certain sense, an opponent of the principle of consent is always in self-contradiction: by choosing a principle of action different from consent he in effect wills not to will. We see here the intrinsic and invincible superiority of democracy over all its competitors. Democracy finds a supporter, indeed an accomplice, in the will of each man as man. The moral prestige and irresistible political strength of democracy derive from its "universalism": man's humanity is the sole "hypothesis" of a democratic regime, and this hypothesis is always verified by us as human beings—unless, of course, we deny outright the humanity of certain people. This is exactly what the totalitarian regimes did, explicitly in the case of Nazism, implicitly or "dialectically" in the case of communism. Nazism subjected or exterminated the "naturally" inferior races; communism subjected or exterminated the "historically" condemned classes.

But how can one fail to see the humanity of another human being? How can it be denied in this terrible way? How could the totalitarian denial of the unity of the human race seem plausible to so many otherwise intelligent people, not all of whom were deliberately evil? I believe that it is because this project was based on certain aspects of being human that are also constitutive of our humanity, on differences that define man as much—or almost as much—as his universal humanity. I speak of the two great differences of nation and class.

Indeed, the contemporary victory of democracy coincides with the weakening in the West of these two differences of nation and class, a weakening due partly to the discredit totalitarianism cast upon them. Today universal humanity tends to overwhelm difference so much that it sometimes seems that between the individual and the world ("we are the world") nothing intrudes except perhaps a void where various ethnic, religious, and sexual "identities" float, each demanding "respect."

It thus seems to me that our feeling about the present situation combines—in different proportions depending on the time, place, and person—satisfaction at the triumph of the democratic principle and anxiety about the disappearance or at least the weakening of all forms of the political articulation of the world, in particular of the nation-state. This last subject will be the focus of the remainder of this essay.

THE REBIRTH OF THE NATION

A historian might say that Europe had already found itself in an analogous situation, one characterized by homogenization. Over two centuries ago, Jean-Jacques Rousseau observed, "Say what you like, there is no such thing nowadays as Frenchmen, Germans, Spaniards, or even Englishmen—only Europeans. All have the same tastes, the same passions, the same customs, and for good reason: Not one of them has ever been formed *nationally,* by distinctive legislation. Put them in the same circumstances, and man for man, they will do exactly the same things."[2]

The Enlightenment—the advent of commerce, of the sciences and arts, and of what soon came to be called "civilization"—produced

2. Jean-Jacques Rousseau, *The Government of Poland*, trans. Willmoore Kendall (Indianapolis: Hackett, 1985), 11.

an initial homogenization of Europe. The French Revolution and its military and ideological consequences, in particular the enormous Napoleonic enterprise, both prolonged the movement toward homogenization and unleashed a contrary movement of particularization and national separation. "I speak for Germans simply, of Germans simply," the philosopher Johann Fichte could declare in 1807, without the enormity of this remark shriveling his tongue in his mouth![3]

To be sure, European nations had existed for a long time, but their particularity now burst forth with a new intensity and energy. They had almost died, or so they felt, but now they believed themselves reborn. And in fact, as a result of the Napoleonic enterprise and its ultimate failure, they *were* reborn. No longer were they merely nations in some passive sense, now they wished *to exist* as nations.

The decisive point to underscore in this context is that democracy and the nation henceforth had a common existence; or, rather, democracy as we understand it came into being within the framework of the nation. The nineteenth century is thus simultaneously the century of democratic expansion and the century of the emergence of nationalities, marked not only by the unification of Italy and Germany but also by various nationalist excesses. On the one hand, democracy multiplied the power of the European nations, whose extraordinary energy was evident in colonial conquests, as well as in the intensity and length of the First World War. On the other hand, the nation provided a concrete context and gave "flesh" to the democratic abstractions of the sovereignty of the people and of the general will. It is this people here who wish to govern themselves, who wish to be represented by a parliament elected by universal suffrage, and so on.

These well-known historical realities lead us to the discussion of

---

3. Johann Gottlieb Fichte, *Addresses to the German Nation*, trans. R. F. Jones and G. H. Turnbull (London: Open Court, 1922), 3. See Rousseau: "It is of man that I must speak, and the question that I examine tells me that I am going to speak to men." *The First and Second Discourses*, ed. Roger D. Masters (New York: St. Martin's, 1964), 101.

a problem of great theoretical and practical interest, a problem that also happens to be the most difficult of all.

Modern democracy, as distinguished from ancient democracy, is not immediately political. It is a principle of legitimacy, that of consent, which was first demanded and which first prevailed in the political order, but which applies to all associations or communities, and thus to all human actions. Alexis de Tocqueville most clearly captures this singular aspect of modern democracy:

> In the United States the dogma of the sovereignty of the people is not an isolated doctrine, bearing no relation to the people's habits and prevailing ideas; on the contrary, one should see it as the last link in a chain of opinions which binds the whole Anglo-American world. Providence has given each individual the amount of reason necessary for him to look after himself in matters of his own exclusive concern. That is the great maxim on which civil and political society in the United States rests; the father of a family applies it to his children, a master to his servants, a township to those under its administration, a province to the townships, a state to the provinces, and the Union to the states. Extended to the nation as a whole, it becomes the dogma of the sovereignty of the people.
>
> Thus, in the United States the generative principle underlying the republic is the same as that which controls the greater part of human actions.[4]

For example, the principle of consent is applicable in the family no less than in the polity, as the evolution of democratic societies attests. In ancient politics, however, democracy presupposed the city, that is, a form, a specific framework, a definite circumscription of humanity. It was the city as city—as a relatively small, homogeneous

---

4. Alexis de Tocqueville, *Democracy in America*, ed. J. P. Mayer, trans. George Lawrence (New York: HarperPerennial, 1988), 397.

civic body capable of being taken in at a glance with one's own eyes ("synoptically," as Aristotle put it)—that made ancient democracy possible, and in a way called it forth. The political problem of modern democracy remained largely unrecognized as long as its national framework was taken for granted, which has been the case since the French Revolution. It is worth noting, however, that in the eighteenth century the democratic principle did not appear under its own name, precisely because the word democracy seemed indissolubly bound to this ancient political form, which long had been considered dead and worthy of little regret.[5] When the authors of *The Federalist* defended and explained the "popular" constitution of the United States, they presented it as a "representative republic" in precise contradistinction to "democracy."[6] Now that the nation has lost its self-evidence, at least in Western Europe, we are rediscovering, although in a different form, the problem that the American Founders faced at the dawn of the democratic nation. The practical political difficulty can be summarized as follows: the democratic principle does not define the framework within which it operates. For example, a vote for self-determination, a democratic act par excellence, takes place within a framework previously established by undemocratic means and principles, generally by tradition, corrected or confirmed by force. Before the French, considering themselves a nation, could take "sovereignty" for themselves in 1789, "forty kings" (as the monarchists said) had first "made France" through marriage and war.

THE AMBIGUITY OF EUROPE

When the nation is weakened and declines as the community of belonging par excellence, the framework in which democracy (and especially popular sovereignty) operates is consequently weakened.

---

5. See Pierre Rosanvallon, "The History of the Word 'Democracy' in France," *Journal of Democracy* 6 (October 1995), 140–54.

6. James Madison, Alexander Hamilton, and John Jay, *The Federalist*, ed. Jacob E. Cooke (Middletown, CT: Wesleyan University Press, 1961), no. 10, 56–65.

One might say that the democratic principle, after having used the nation as an instrument or vehicle, abandons it by the wayside. This would not be worrisome if a new vehicle were available or clearly under construction. This new political form, however, is nowhere in sight. Of course, some might suggest that "Europe" is this new political framework. In a certain sense this is true. After the Second World War the European idea and its accompanying institutions facilitated the reconstruction on solid foundations of the European nation-state, while also making plausible, imaginable, and even desirable the withering away of this supposedly antiquated political form. But does "Europe" mean today the depoliticization of the life of peoples—that is, the increasingly methodical reduction of their collective existence to the activities of "civil society" and the mechanisms of "civilization"? Or does it instead entail the construction of a new political body, a great, enormous European nation? The construction of Europe, from the Common Market established in 1957 to the European Union today, has made progress only because of this ambiguity, and as a result of combining these two contradictory projects it has taken on its character as an imperious, indefinite, and opaque movement. Thus, this initially happy ambiguity has become paralyzing, and threatens soon to become fatal. The sleepwalker's assurance with which "Europe" pursues its indefinite extension is the result of its obstinate refusal to think about itself comprehensively—that is, to define itself politically.

Europe refuses to define itself politically. What precisely does this mean? A political order is a public or common thing (*res publica*) and therefore a certain way of "putting something or having something in common." The first thing a political order puts in common is a certain territory and a certain population. Democracy requires that the population consent to the political structure proposed to it. But what population should we ask for consent—in this case, whether it wishes to belong to Europe? Why ask, for example, the Swedes, but not the Moroccans, who, after all, are more familiar to us French?

The political vacuity of Europe was harshly brought to light by the recent war in the former Yugoslavia. The territorial "unconsciousness" of our Europe, its refusal to take seriously the problem of territory and population as a political question, finds its counterpart—and its nemesis—in the other Europe, where the ethnic cleansers worked with utmost savagery to make population and territory coincide. Refusing to consider the territorial question as important in itself—incapable, in fact, of seeing, feeling, and conceiving its own territory—Europe understands passionate attachment to a place as folly, which is exactly what the behavior of the ethnic cleansers confirms. Europe does not understand that if it wants to think and to act politically, it first must think and will a definite territorial arrangement, both within and beyond its borders. After much lost time, such an arrangement was finally imposed in the former Yugoslavia by the United States, the "imperial," that is, the political power par excellence. As we know, in order to achieve this result it was necessary at the Dayton peace talks to reproduce the "virtual" image of the *territory* of Bosnia-Herzegovina!

I do not think it necessary to multiply examples in order to confirm the importance, even today, of territory and more generally of political forms and parameters. Yet however numerous these examples may be, they do not forestall an objection that comes immediately to mind: politics, as the putting of things in common, or giving form to what a certain number of people have in common, is outdated. The network of "communications" is now so dense and extensive that humanity as a whole possesses a *sensorium commune* sufficient for all its legitimate needs. In this network, each one can find his place at the intersection of a multiplicity of identities—familial, local, sexual, and so on—that can be almost infinitely combined. There is little doubt that this is the direction our world seems to have taken. It is not absurd to think, therefore, that political attachments (foremost among them, national passions) are deplorably archaic ways for individuals and groups to select their identities. Moreover, do not the various nationalisms of today, which even when they are violent tend to be defensive rather than expansive, seem to confirm that they belong to the past?

THE LIMITS OF "COMMUNICATION"

The recollection of an older Europe—a homogeneous Europe, and one without passports!—that nevertheless exploded into furiously inimical nations ought to move us to prudence. "Communication" by itself does not create a true bond among people. It is like an amorous encounter reduced to the "kiss" of two telephone numbers on a computer screen. Today's popular term *identity* is a terribly impoverished substitute for the older term *community*. Among the communities that make up the human world, the political community was traditionally considered to be the community par excellence, the "supreme" community, as Aristotle famously noted in his *Politics* (1252a–b). The question is thus inevitably raised: Do people necessarily need a "community par excellence"? And supposing that they can and want to do without such a community, would their lives as a result be freer and richer, or rather the opposite? I do not have the space here to respond to these questions other than by a series of assertions.

Man as a free and rational being cannot fulfill himself except in a political community, with all the consequences (not all of them pleasant) that this entails. It is in the political body, and only in the political body, that we seriously put things in common. And we are obliged "to put things in common" in order to realize our membership in the same species, in order to concretize our universal humanity. Why? Why not be content with the family—whether nuclear or extended—supplemented by the local community, and perhaps by the new "family" that individuals today find in their business or workplace? Without insisting on the fact that the family today is less and less a community, I would observe merely that however one might conceive of the family's vocation or purpose (if it has one), the family is rooted in the particularity of bodies, in the needs and desires of our animal nature. Its law is love; its emotional tone is one of unmediated identification. It therefore leaves the individual short of justice, which presupposes or requires rational deliberation. The political community is thus irreplaceable as the framework for deliberation over justice. This deliberation is serious because it has real consequences: the taxes I pay, the laws I obey, perhaps even the war I am obliged to fight. In short, the meaning of the city is precisely not to be the family. In the city all of the individual's faculties come into play. In the city people "put in common actions and reasons," as Aristotle puts it in his *Nichomachean Ethics* (1126b11–12).

IDENTITY VERSUS IDENTIFICATION

It is for this general reason—and not primarily to provide a rationalization for my own national passion, which is undoubtedly quite real—that I argue that we should show more respect, not for "identity," which is a passive, lifeless notion easily manipulated by demagogues, but for the political bodies that are the political contexts of human action. In Europe, this means the nation. Let me add that if one thinks of the nation in political terms, as the political context of action rather than as a "cultural identity" to be defended, then its relationship to the "European project" ceases to be as conflictual as either stubborn nationalists or fervent supranationalists believe.[7]

---

7. I would note in passing that the notion of "cultural identity" is, in this context, both inconsistent and violent. It erases the articulations of the human world by jumbling together religion, the arts, principles of government, mores and private manners, and the like. To be sure, it is legitimate to think that these diverse elements, variously combined, give to each political body a "general spirit" that the legislator should respect. This is Montesquieu's position, and it contains nothing inconsistent or violent. But these elements, from which the "general spirit" of the nation is distilled, are ultimately held together by its political form. Once this form is effaced—whether or not it is replaced by another—the distillate evaporates like perfume from a broken bottle. If, for example, we suppose that France were to disappear as a political body, then a serious French Catholic would no longer have any "metafamilial" tie except to the Catholic Church—and certainly not to the abstraction called "French culture"!

Instead of speaking of "identity," which is passive and passé, let us speak of "identification," which is active and, I dare say, a call to action. Europe cannot construct itself meaningfully (i.e., politically) unless Europeans in the various nations identify themselves with a common European political action, and for the foreseeable future that means with the common action of European nations. Someone might say that this proposition is tautological. I do not think so. It acknowledges these two characteristics of real life: first of all, politics is about action; and second, the motive of action is the future or a view of the future. Here one may object that I am only reformulating the old saw of "political voluntarism," which condemns us to the kind of pious exhortations that are received with more and more irritation by European peoples. However, by refraining from defining the European identity and by calling for political action, we do not opt for something arbitrary and condemn ourselves to impotence. There already exists a certain tradition of common European action to which we can appeal. The moral-political root of the construction of Europe was the decision taken by France and Germany in the 1950s, and later ratified and deepened by Charles de Gaulle and Konrad Adenauer between 1958 and 1963, to consider each other as partners, allies, and even friends. This politically decisive decision was made by nations and not by a supranational institution. It in no way required any previous accord on some "European cultural identity." This is not the place to develop this point in terms of political objectives or programs. I merely want to suggest that to speak of common political action by European nations is a proposition that is quite meaningful, one that invites us to extend into the future what Michael Oakeshott would have called an "idiom of conduct."

DEMOCRACY WITHOUT A BODY?

If we do not succeed in tightening the dangerously loosening bonds in the Western world between human communities and the political action of their governments, the divorce between the nation and democracy will be no less dangerous for democracy than for the nation. What is a democracy without a body, a democracy deprived of what psychologists call the sentiment of one's own body? With respect to the principle of democracy, its territorial framework is external, contingent, and thus arbitrary. That is why as democracy today grows more and more self-aware and self-confident, it so tranquilly bids farewell to the nation, the framework that seemed natural to it for two centuries. Democracy punishes the nation for the follies it caused it to commit, but also, one fears, for the services the nation once rendered it (which reveals a more than royal ingratitude). Modern democracy, which is founded on the will, wants to be self-sufficient, but it cannot do without a body. Yet how can it give itself a new body, a body that would not be the necessarily contingent and arbitrary legacy of the predemocratic age, a body of which democracy would be the sole author? Therefore, democracy has put on this abstract body called "Europe." But in order for this body to become real, and to be able to produce and circumscribe an awareness of itself, it must have height, length, depth, and dimensions—that is, limits. But since every limit would be arbitrary from the point of view of the democratic principle, democracy gives itself a body without limits: a Europe of indefinite extension, a Europe contradictorily defined as indefinite extension. How many nations, in fact, belong to it? Twelve? Twenty? Thirty? Does Turkey, for example, belong? Why not? Or why? The European political class has not even seriously begun to ask these questions, let alone answer them.

The world of democratic nations was formed when the principle of consent was adopted by political bodies that had been constituted in accord with other principles, both political and religious. Now that the principle of consent has banished every other principle, it is not clear how a new body could form and then subject itself to the principle of consent that constituted the democratic nation. The political molds are broken, and democratic vigilance inhibits their reconstruction. Instead of vigilance, it would perhaps be better to speak of arrogance and immoderation. Indeed, democracy may be starting to suffer the consequences of the immoderation that has characterized it for the last generation. Perhaps the political impotence I have tried to describe is the punishment inflicted on Europeans for accepting only the principle of consent as legitimate, for using the principle of freedom in a tyrannical fashion. The European wanted only what he himself willed; he rejected as arbitrary and outdated the nation, the political instrument that allowed him, by giving him limits, to exercise his sovereignty or will. Now his will finds itself increasingly without an instrument, without a framework of formation and action, alone and politically impotent. Even with the meticulously guaranteed democratic right to will everything, the European as a citizen finds himself able to accomplish less and less.

I have spoken of democracy's "punishment" of the nation. One might prefer another word. For the point of view I am defending here is not the moral or religious one that reproaches modern man for having rejected natural or divine law. Rather, my perspective is political. Whatever man's latitude to define and to produce his conditions of existence, he is not the sovereign author of the human world. It is therefore dangerous, and above all logically contradictory, for him to act as if he were its sovereign author—which is precisely what he does when he grants exclusive legitimacy to the principle of consent. We do not reflect enough on the singular fact that we are the first people who wish to submit all the aspects of the world to a single principle. Even though this principle is that of liberty, the project itself nonetheless has something tyrannical about it. Two and a half centuries ago, when religious rule was burdensome and even in certain ways tyrannical, the great French liberal political philosopher Montesquieu, perhaps the most judicious defender of modern liberty, wrote: "It is strange to say, tho' true, that virtue itself has need of limits."[8] Today, the true friends of liberty are

---

8. Montesquieu, *The Spirit of the Laws: A Compendium of the First English Edition with an English Translation of "An Essay on Causes Affecting Mind and Character,"* ed. David W. Carrithers, trans. Thomas Nugent (Berkeley, CA: University of California Press, 1978), bk. 11, ch. 4.

inclined to think, even if they do not yet dare to state, "Who would say it! Liberty itself has need of limits." These limits include those of the political body, for only within the political body can liberty be truly effective.

One might say that if man is a political animal (as is obviously presupposed by my remarks), his political nature will not allow itself to be rendered impotent. It inevitably will find some way of asserting itself in an unprecedented manner. I believe this too. But in a world where the principle of consent increasingly is becoming a principle of political impotence and paralysis, the only other principle capable of constructing political institutions, or at least of producing political effects, will be the unprincipled principle of pure force. This is a principle that lacks any spiritual dimension and completely disregards consent. (By the way, it is because force disregards the principle of consent that, in certain circumstances, it obtains it most easily.)

A political body always combines force and justice in variable proportions. As soon as there is a political body, justice is never wholly without force. But if we completely leave behind political existence we must fear that, despite all the cultural, commercial, and technological artifices of a perfected civilization, justice and force might find themselves completely separated, with justice becoming perfectly pure or impotent and force merely strong or unjust. Our old nations, it is true, are tired, unwieldy, slow to move, obtuse, and pretentious. But they are also substantial and enduring; they are infinitely precious "condensations" of thoughts and actions; above all, they are still the only political entity that we have between us and "the state of nature," or, rather, between us and this state of civilization without justice. It is not by ceaselessly denigrating these nations but only by employing their energy, dormant but still capable of being roused, that we have the possibility of elaborating a new political body, a political "Europe" that will not succumb to the first storm over monetary or defense policy.

THE PARTICULAR AND THE UNIVERSAL

If the preceding might be seen as a defense of the nation, it is of the nation as a political body and not as an expression of particularity. To defend the nation in its particularity is ultimately to condemn it as only a region, a territory, or (even less than a territory) a "culture." Thus understood, the nation has only the ineffable but paltry charm of "the people from here," and about the people from here one can only say, in the words of a popular French song, "They're from here, the people from here." On the other hand, as a political body the nation in Europe has succeeded in a manner comparable only to the ancient city in realizing the articulation of the particular and the universal. Each great action and each great thought produced by one of our nations was a challenge to and a proposal for the other nations, a proposal by humanity for humanity. But like the Greek cities, our nations ended up succumbing to the intensity with which each asserted its part in what Shakespeare called the "great quarrel."

Today the nation's power to articulate the universal on the basis of the particular is weakening, and the two are coming apart. On one side, we see the particularity inseparable from all real human things; on the other, the universal is becoming the general, that is, this unreal "communication" that pretends to be real, as if the unity of humankind had already been realized through such superficial ties. I am told that in Switzerland the great "national" languages, especially German, are less and less in use among the young because they have lost their prestige in favor of the local dialect on the one hand and worldwide "English" on the other. The concrete universal of the national-cum-universal language has given way to the sterile juxtaposition of the patois of the "people from here" and the impoverished, "brutal" language of people from nowhere. If things continue in this fashion the phenomenon will soon extend throughout Europe. A national language cannot be preserved and reanimated unless it is the instrument by which the nation proposes something for humanity at large and, first of all, for Europe. It must be an instrument for larger national and political purposes. It cannot merely serve the subpolitical task of promoting commerce and communication.

I am sure that these remarks will appear to many enlightened minds to be excessively emotional. My hope, however, is at least to have shown that one may still "defend the nation" out of concern not for the particular but rather for the universal.

APPENDIX B: WHAT IS A NATION?

IT IS CERTAINLY imprudent to begin a lecture by asking a question, since the audience is then justified in expecting an answer.[1] However imprudent, to give an answer to this question is precisely what I am going to try to do. I do not expect that you will all be convinced by my answer. But I would be disappointed if I did not convince you of the importance of this question. If we do not reach some clarity about it, then we will be less and less able to meet the present and imminent political challenges, and we will eventually lose our way.

This question is rarely posed, however. Generally speaking, we are not keen to ask this kind of question. We do not spontaneously ask *what* a thing is, although we freely expatiate on how good or how bad it is. This is especially the case when addressing political things. Sometimes the nation is considered as a good thing, perhaps even the best human thing; sometimes the nation is considered as a bad thing, perhaps even the worst political thing. In either case there is not much motivation to explore the *what*—the nature—of the nation.

---

1. This lecture was originally given in Munich in 2006 at the Carl Friedrich von Siemens Stiftung.

In my country, the question was asked and answered by Ernest Renan in 1882. In his famous lecture of that year titled "Qu'est-ce qu'une nation?" he addressed it in a way that made his answer determinative for modern French self-consciousness. This was a time when the nation was considered the ultimate form of political life; thus, it was not a very propitious time for a serious study of its nature. But the French nation had just suffered a humiliating defeat at the hands of Prussia, and as a consequence the German empire had just been founded. So the strong—indeed, enthusiastic—general adherence to the nation as such was mitigated by the despondency and anxiety of this nation at this particular juncture. There was an opening for the mind. In his 1882 lecture, Renan formulated in a scholarly and moderate tone the views he had expressed more pungently in letters written to David Friedrich Strauss during and immediately after the Franco-Prussian War.

Putting his argument in a nutshell: Renan opposed the French and German ideas of the nation, the latter resting on the brute facts of race and language, the former on the free will of particular populations. He then compared the existence of the nation to *un plébiscite de tous les jours,* "a quotidian or daily plebiscite." However striking the contrast, though, this stark opposition fails to completely convince. Not only did it provide a reverse image of the relative situation of the two nations under consideration—one cannot help thinking that the country defeated on the battlefield gets her revenge in the realm of ideas. But furthermore, however sympathetic we are today to Renan's thesis—and the German reader no less and perhaps more so than the French one—we cannot fail to notice that for a nation to exist it needs the "German" no less than the "French" element. However "open" a nation may be, the word "nation" itself suggests that it is defined above all by its "children" being born on its soil.[2] A nation is first of all a motherland or a *Vaterland,* a *patrie.* The specific work of the nation is to join and as it were to fuse the brute fact of birth with the free adhesion of the

---

2. "Nation" comes from the Latin *nasci,* which means to be born or generated. (Trans.)

heart and mind. Renan would not deny this, but his defining the nation merely by opposing two different conceptions is far from sufficient if we intend to grasp firmly *what it is*.

That was a long time ago. We no longer think, like Renan and his contemporaries, that the nation is the most perfect form of human association. For the last half-century in Europe we have even engaged in a huge enterprise aimed implicitly or even deliberately at the definitive overcoming of our European nations. After three Franco-German wars, two of which have engulfed the world, it seems we have no more use for the French than we do for the German idea of the nation. But then it would seem that this is a good time for the philosophic bird again to take flight: the nation has become all that it could be, so we are finally in a position to grasp what it is. Alas, the conviction that the nation is the main culprit in the catastrophes of the twentieth century prevents us from seriously trying. Since we are so certain it is bad, why bother to inquire into its nature? Therefore, instead of asking about the nation, most political scientists today study nationalism, understood as the phenomenon that uniquely reveals the nation's essence. This procedure is all the more attractive since the noun already includes a judgment and condemnation. Once we have started down this path, all efforts at an impartial inquiry are fruitless. Of course, one could object that we have no need for impartiality in these matters, that exercising this virtue here could even be vicious, if it encourages present-day citizens to cling to this calamitous form of political life. What could be the utility for our political life of an ample and accurate knowledge of the nation? We are thus tempted to "forget about it."

I do not think that we can indulge in this sort of avoidance or consignment to oblivion. Among the many reasons I could adduce, the following is sufficient. After more than a half-century of trying, the European enterprise, the effort "to construct Europe," has not succeeded in overcoming our old nations. And nobody expects it will succeed any time soon. For all practical purposes, the frame of our lives will retain a national character for the foreseeable future. Our nations are here to stay for a while longer. To be sure, they are now and will be in the future very different from what they were at the time of Renan and Strauss. But this complex of facts means that it is incumbent on us to investigate the nature of the nation. Even if we are to live in nations that will be mere shadows of their former selves, we need to know what they were when they were really themselves.

In this way an unexpected yet reassuring constellation begins to take shape: Europe and its nations appear less and less as opposite and exclusive forms of political association—with the former irresistibly taking the place of the latter. Rather, they are interdependent and inseparable modalities of an enormous, still unfinished, and rather mysterious historical phenomenon. In any event the idea is dawning on us that what we call a nation is the political form proper to Europe, since it was produced by a complex of circumstances and purposes exclusive to it and its American offspring.

BEFORE THE NATION: FROM THE CITY TO EMPIRE

However plausible or at least intriguing these reflections may be, they do not provide us with the wherewithal to begin to address the question that forms the title of this lecture. Until now we have stayed among the nations, so to speak, letting ourselves be guided by some differences between them—for instance between France and Germany as discussed by Renan. But this ultimately has failed to yield a sure and adequate way back to the object of our inquiry. We need to take a step back. As you will soon see, it will of necessity be a major step back.

We need to look at the nation *from the outside*. How can we do this, since we have lived in nations from time immemorial? Thankfully, our Western memory is longer than our respective national memories. At least intellectually, we have access to other political forms we can press into service for a systematic comparison with the nation. Luckily, the number of political forms is not indefinite. Indeed, it is very small. As far as they interest us politically, their number is no greater than three. In addition to the nation, and for the purpose of a defining comparison, we need to take into account only two other political forms, the city and the empire.

The city and the empire are the political forms characteristic of Greek and Roman antiquity. Chronologically, and perhaps genetically, they come *before* our nations. This chronological advantage is compounded by a logical advantage: they are easier to define than the nation.

Let us begin with the city. Of the three political forms under consideration, it is the only one for which we can give a complete, and thus a completely satisfactory, definition. The city is particularly susceptible to being defined because it is constituted by its *fines*, by its limits. In Leo Strauss's felicitous formulation, "the *polis* is that complete association which corresponds to the natural range of man's power of knowing and of loving."[3] In such a definition the *ought* is included in the *is*. But let us also listen to the best analyst of the ancient city: "the best defining principle for a city is this: the greatest number of members with a view to self-sufficiency of life that is readily surveyable."[4] We need to keep in mind this defining trait of the city: the city is readily surveyable, it is *eusunoptos*.

The empire is less easy to define because in contrast to the city its defining trait is its limitlessness. Far from being *eusunoptos*, it extends well beyond the horizon. To be grasped it requires the imagination, which it stirs and even inflames. You could retort that with all this indeterminacy, the empire implies a clear definition inasmuch as the notion points toward an all-encompassing gathering of all peoples under one rule—ultimately, the gathering

---

3. See *Natural Right and History* (Chicago: University of Chicago Press [1953], 1974), 254n2.
4. See Aristotle's *Politics*, 1326b, trans. Carnes Lord (Chicago: University of Chicago Press, 1985), 205.

of the whole human race, all humankind, under the same rule. The objection is valid, except for the fact that this gathering of all men, contrary to the civic association, is an imagined gathering: the most extended empires in history have left out large segments of humanity. Thus, practically speaking, the notion of empire is a performative one; it involves the impulse and efforts to attain the greatest possible extension of a domination. Aiming ultimately to gather the entire human race, which is humanly impossible, it tends beyond humanity. Only a superhuman ruler would be able to govern the human race. The emperor has to have a godly or divine nature.

Empires are able and likely to be found in all parts of the world and all civilizations. In China, in Africa, in Central America, in ancient and modern Europe—one could go on and on. This is not the case with the city. However especially *natural* it may be (as Aristotle argued in the *Politics*), the city has fully developed only in the European domain broadly understood—that is, from the Greek *poleis* through the cities of northern Italy and northern Europe to the *townships* of New England discussed by Tocqueville. What I stated earlier is therefore in need of correction: the empire and city are the political forms characterizing Greek and Roman antiquity inasmuch as the empires came after, and in some sense rested upon, a previous civic life. This was not the case with the other empires to which I have alluded.

Of course, the articulation of the empire and city differed in the cases of the Hellenistic empire and the Roman empire. However dependent the former was on the Greek idea of the human species, however dependent Alexander was on Aristotle (even though the youngster's political application of the idea did not receive the master's approbation), the Macedonian empire superimposed itself on the Greek cities without radically transforming them. In the case of Rome, on the contrary, the empire was born from the city, from the entrails of the city it eventually tore apart. Although you probably have the impression that I have set out to discourse on everything under the sun, I will mostly skip this—admittedly huge—speck of the Roman empire. Let me briefly sketch what interests me about Rome in this inquiry into the genesis and nature of the nation.

It is worth asking what made Rome so fascinating in the centuries following its demise, since much of what had happened in the name of "Rome" was of unparalleled squalor and ugliness. Different answers are possible and legitimate. I submit this one: Rome fascinates because it underwent the greatest political transformation ever seen. The Greek cities—especially Athens—had undergone profound transformations, from the city of the Eupatrides to the city of "the ultimate demos."[5] One could argue that classical political science came into being for the purpose of understanding political change, more precisely the change of regime. But however deep and significant these changes were, they did not touch the political form itself; they did not affect the city as such. Athens submitted to Philip of Macedon while retaining its form as a city. Rome, on the contrary, underwent a complete transformation as a political form; from a city it became an empire, a change of form that of course included a change of regime.

What is most fascinating in this fascinating story is the protracted, convulsive, and bloody process of transition between the two forms. A standard and convenient way to shed light on this process is to understand it as a conflict between two regimes, an aristocratic republic on one hand, and an absolute monarchy on the other, embodied respectively by two extraordinary men, Cato and Caesar. However enlightening it may be, this interpretation leaves out much of importance. One can get at its omissions by asking the Plutarchian question: What made the great men of Rome different from the great men of Greece? In Greece, even in Athens, these were willing to offer their services to the Great King or to another city when crossed by their fellow citizens. But however willing they were, they could not control the forces of the

---

5. Manent has in mind Aristotle's discussion in *The Constitution of Athens*. (Trans.)

city independently from the regime of the city. In Rome, on the other hand, the energies of the republic detached themselves from the senatorial regime. After that time, they were, so to speak, at the disposal of the one able to handle them. Think of Caesar's conquest of the Gauls, which he single-handedly pursued for nearly a decade not only without the approbation but also against the mind of the senate. The German historian Christian Meier's convincing thesis is that the difference between Sulla and Pompey on the one hand, and Caesar on the other, lies in the former having retained some respect for the senatorial regime (if not for the senators themselves: Sulla can be said to have reformed the senatorial regime against the grain of the senate). Caesar, however, felt no less contempt for the regime than for the persons of the senate. Did Caesar deliberately aim at founding another regime, a monarchical one? The question is perhaps moot, and not only because he died before he was forced to show his hand. We get the distinct impression that he simply enacted his sovereignty without bothering to give an account of it.

One of the main causes of the separation of the forces of the city from its regime was a blurring of the difference between inside and outside, citizen and foreigner. This blurring came to a head in the first century B.C. during the War with the Allies about their getting full rights as Roman citizens.[6] Sulla was the first to enter Rome as a conqueror and to treat his fellow citizens as he would the worst enemies of Rome. He thus prepared Caesar's crossing of the Rubicon.

The European tradition, even the republican one, did not simply side with the republican killers of Caesar. This was because Caesar did not simply embody monarchy, or despotism, or tyranny, as opposed to a republic or a free regime. Paradoxically, his personal, quasi-divine ascendancy and domination rested upon, and brought to ultimate fruition, a "republican" confidence in one's own forces. Blurring the opposition between republican self-government and monarchical domination, Caesar embodied and consummated

---

6. In America this is often called "the Social War" (91–88 B.C.). "Social" comes from the Latin word *socius/socii*, or ally; it is the root of the word "associate." (Trans.)

pagan pride. Among the numerous titles borne by the pope in Rome, none is more beautiful than *servus servorum Dei* (servant of the servants of God). To the titles that have been piled on Caesar's head, I propose, somewhat belatedly, that we add the following: *Dominus dominorum mundi* (Lord of the lords of the world).

THE CHURCH AND EUROPE'S NEW POLITICAL FORM

We are a long way from home but we haven't lost our way. We needed to give a sketch of the ancient pagan dynamism and trajectory because these provide us the broadest and most direct access to the natural order of political things. During the first centuries of the Christian dispensation and for quite a long time afterward, city and empire were the only available political forms. Cities *naturally* grew up, particularly, as I have recalled, in northern Italy and northern Europe. And the prestige of the Roman empire was such that a Holy Roman German empire evolved in western Europe. However, despite this imperial prestige, despite the magnificent flowering of so many cities from Florence through Venice to Cologne and Amsterdam, the most significant fact of our history is that Europe did not organize itself durably in the form of cities or an empire. Instead, it was forced to produce a radically new political form. The way to break the standoff between city and empire, between Guelphs and Ghibellines, was to invent a political form unknown to the ancients. This, as you no doubt have divined, was the nation, the European nation, the political form that is so familiar to us.

The ancient or natural conflict between city and empire, therefore, did not issue in the ancient or natural outcomes, whether the victory of one or a complex equilibrium between the two. The old dynamics no longer ruled, no longer produced the accustomed order or disorder. Why? A third party—not a political one—had introduced itself, purporting to mediate the conflict or tension between city and empire. I allude to the Catholic Church, of course. The church is not strictly a political form, but it introduced such a

95

deep reconsideration and recomposition of human association that it would be prudent to include it among the political forms, if only never to lose sight of the part it played in constituting the European political landscape, especially through its role in giving birth to the political form proper—even exclusive—to Europe: the nation. I have already been brazen enough to give an account of pagan or natural politics in a few pages. I have at my disposal even less space to sketch the political significance and effects of the church. Well, it is too late to bow out now.

In some politically relevant sense, the church is stronger than either the city or the empire. It is stronger for spiritual reasons, which have political consequences. The church, as a purported perfect society—if you prefer, as an imagined perfect society—undermines the moral components and conditions of the city and the empire as human associations. Through the specific characteristic animating it—that is, through charity—the church goes deeper than the city and further than the empire. The mere notion of charity—love of the neighbor for the love of God—opens up perspectives and possibilities that are enough to reorder the way we look at the human association.

Now, without entering into the question of the virtues and the vices of the church, it is enough to remark that the church, as its founder said, is not of this world. It is, or was, essentially unable to make charity the animating principle of our political associations. If you do not believe me, I am sure you will believe Machiavelli, who explained that the church in Italy was too strongly opposed to the profane institutions but too weak to be able to replace them. Here is the heart of the matter. The church decisively and definitively changed the way Europeans looked at the human association, and thus it decisively and definitively transformed the conditions of their political life, but without ever being in a position to govern them politically. On the hoary subject of the relation between politics and religion in Europe, the most important point, to my mind, is the following: in the whole course of our history, the church or

Christianity never governed Europeans *politically*, including during the period when the Roman Church claimed for itself the *plenitudo potestatis*, the plenitude of power. The proposition is familiar to us through the polemical formulations of modern philosophers from Machiavelli through Hobbes to Rousseau, all of whom affirmed that the political contribution of Christianity is, in Rousseau's formulation, "to make impossible any good political regime in the Christian States." Stripped of its polemical or anti-Christian edge, the proposition is all the more enlightening and true.

The incompatibility between the church on the one hand and the city and the empire on the other goes both ways. The church is stronger than either the city or the empire because it goes deeper than the city and further than the empire. Conversely, the city is peculiarly inimical to the church because its civic passions bend the human heart toward human affairs, while the empire also is inimical to the church because it entertains (competing) universal claims. To summarize: our forebears had at their disposal three modes of human association, three political forms that could neither be reconciled nor made compatible. How did the nation evolve from such a hopeless situation? How did a nation-based order develop from this chaos? I do not underestimate the role of subpolitical factors—of geography, languages, mores, etc. But these belong to what Aristotle would call "material causes"; as such, they do not give access to the form—to this unprecedented political form. The nation could come into being only through the action of the form itself, of what is the most formal in the form—that is, its unity. The entering wedge of the nation-to-be was the Christian king. The European nation came into being through obedience to the Christian king.

THE CHRISTIAN KING

Just as the defects of city and empire in their relation to the church go both ways, the advantages of the Christian king also go in both directions. He is more acceptable to the church than either the citizen-body of a city or an emperor. Citizens are carried away by passions that make them forgetful of their souls, while the emperor aims at a *plenitudo potestatis* that necessarily rivals that which is claimed by the church. In contrast, the Christian king bends the will of his subjects toward obedience, thus disposing them to obey the law of God and the injunctions of the church. At the same time, the extension of his power is confined within the limits of his realm, thereby conceding to the church her exclusive claim to universality. Conversely, this king—who in these ways is quite agreeable to the church—is in a position to defend the prerogatives of the secular domain against the encroachments of the church. He can do so much more efficiently than the republican citizen-body, which is always prone to agitation and disruption by the promises and threats of the church. He is also more effective than the emperor, whose unwieldy domain is even less susceptible to a rational government. Thus, the Christian king appears as a historical agent of great magnitude. He can cooperate with the apostolic mission of the church (think of Alexander VI's 1493 bull giving the Spanish crown an apostolic quality and mission in the Indies), while striving mightily to have his government freed as far as possible from its demands.

I readily admit that, however valid, this short description of the Christian king is very far from giving us a sufficient grasp of the nation of which he was the head. At the very most, we have limned a fairly suggestive idea of the formative soul of the European nation (let us think, for example, of Joan of Arc having Charles VII crowned at Reims). But what of its body? After all, we speak of "political bodies," not "political souls."

However addicted to inference and deduction I may appear, I do not intend to deduce the bodies of the European nations from their kingly souls! Innumerable circumstances, both natural and human, contributed to their extraordinary variety. More important, the contingent character of their bodies belongs to their essence:

they are a kind of mean between the powerful localism of the city (a Florentine citizen is loath to venture very far from the Ponte Vecchio) and the imperial impulse to look toward unsubdued regions beyond the horizon (there is always an expedition being prepared against the Parthians).

This does not mean that these bodies were simply divorced from their souls. The faculties of the latter played their roles, including what one might call "the national imagination." The national imagination has this singular character of being at once quite ample and neatly circumscribed, a reflection of which is to be found in our meticulously drawn national boundaries. In this connection I submit this thesis, or rather, hypothesis: this searching for the mean, this circumscribing of the national imagination, presupposed and built upon Christian qualities. Because every human being is my neighbor, charity alleviates the pressure of those who are naturally close to me while it draws closer those who live far away; it weakens the grasp of localism while it assuages the vertigo of faraway domination. Again, I am not suggesting that charity as a theological virtue directly produced these political effects, only that whether the virtue was effective or not the perspective derived from charity informed the imagination of our forefathers and helped them discover a middle dimension between the little and the immense, thus preparing their souls for the nation that was then in formation.

Although this kind of analysis does not point toward particular events or a neatly determined period, it nevertheless aims to shed some light on a long and confused development. During its course, Christian kings and princes tried to enforce a more and more exact obedience, while the *corps* of their subjects, circumscribed more and more neatly, was feeling its way toward self-awareness—that is, toward *national* self-awareness.

THE CHRISTIAN NATION AND THE "MIDDLE DIMENSION"

Then came the crisis, the contentious joining together of soul and body, of obedience and fellow feeling. I refer to the crisis of the Reformation period. In the context of these reflections, the Reformation appears as the period of the nationalization of Christianity—or, more precisely, of the national appropriation of Christianity. The translation of the Bible into national languages served as the most revealing and effective instrument of this appropriation. The national appropriation of Christianity was necessarily a subjective appropriation. Only through the crystallizing of the nation can Christian liberty coincide with Christian obedience. At that time, Christendom was broken apart and the "commonwealth of Christian subjects," the Christian nation, was born.

The pivotal role of the Christian king shows itself in the fact that he (or indeed she) morphed into, or prepared the way for, or had to make way for the secular, neutral, or as Hobbes put it, the "abstract" state. Indeed, Hobbes—the most sober, reasonable, and persuasive enemy of the Christian name in European history—is a credible witness to the truth of the thesis I seek to defend. He offered to put an end to the disorders resulting from the Reformation, or which the Reformation had not healed, by founding a new political form *exclusively* on the previously unheard-of basis of the absolute unity of command. As he made admirably clear, solutions deriving from the two great Roman experiences—republican liberty and imperial-Catholic authority—as well as from the evangelical or Protestant confidence in individual grace made the disease more virulent rather than curing it. He therefore proposed a science of obedience "built upon sure and clear principles." He proposed the modern state, for which he drew up the plan. He grasped with perfect clarity that this state would mean the end of the church as it had been understood up to then. He wrote the following: "And therefore a Church, such a one as is capable to command, to judge, absolve, condemn, or do any other act, is the same thing with a civil Commonwealth, consisting of Christian men; and is called a *civil State*, for that the subjects of it are *men*; and a *Church*, for that the subjects thereof are *Christians*."[7] But if Europe was composed of "commonwealths consisting of Christians," then the sovereign, neutral, abstract state was concretely in need of a Christian commonwealth, also known as a Christian *nation*.

Now, if we go back to the point from where we started, we understand that the conjunction of a neutral state and a Christian nation finally solved the "Roman problem," which had never ceased to be *our* problem. Since the beginning of the first century B.C., the Romans had been caught and torn between the republican city and the monarchical empire, between a rather narrowly limited natural body politic (remember Strauss's characterization of the city) and an enormous, indeed limitless one. That was the problem of political physics we needed to solve, without having recourse to the imperial solution the Christian church had robbed of its legitimacy. As I have tried to argue, Europeans distributed themselves among a plurality of large but limited political bodies that were made possible and in some sense necessary by the pressure of the Christian affirmation.

I need not prolong the story by describing how, after the Christian king had given way to the sovereign and neutral state, the national-Christian fellow feeling became less and less Christian and more and more "purely national"; how the political imagination of most European nations caught fire at the thought of the endless territories lying beyond the horizon, with their benighted populations waiting to be baptized, civilized, or simply exploited; how, as the nineteenth century was drawing to a close, new imperial ideas of class or race superseded the national imaginations. Soon nationalist—or rather imperialist Europe—would destroy itself.

And where are we now? We are back to square one, in the sense that we again confront the meaning of the European nation *as such*, shorn of nationalist or imperialist fantasies and pretensions.

---

7. See *Leviathan*, ch. 39, in fine.

More precisely, whether we are French or Germans, Italians or Spaniards, we no longer define ourselves as belonging to Christian nations. We have discarded, or at least greatly curtailed, the claim to national sovereignty; we have even agreed to erase our borders, which had been meticulously drawn and passionately defended until not so long ago. And as I speak, we ask ourselves—situated uncomfortably between our rump nations and a half-baked Europe—whether to go further in the direction of a limitless European empire of universal fellow feeling, or to stop at this point and confront our necessities, or perhaps even to go back a little and try to breathe new life into our old nations. We are not sure after all that it is possible or desirable to live a "postnational" life.

Thus we are caught again in the "Roman syndrome." We are torn between the opposite directions of the imagination I tried to describe. On the one hand, we experience the passion for the little platoon, morally much smaller indeed than the ancient city, since it is deprived of political self-government; on the other hand, we experience the imperial urge toward what is beyond the horizon, beyond the borders of Europe, however defined. We are fast losing the middle dimension, with its inseparable physical and spiritual aspects, on which we predicated everything that is still worthy of being cherished in our several national histories as well as in our common European history. In this sense, I think that we are on the verge of self-destruction. To parry this threat, nothing is more important than to get an effective grip on our centuries-old development. And that means first of all that we must again become fully aware of the original Christian character of our nations. As should be clear by now, this claim entails not the slightest suggestion for a rollback of the secular state: in fact, as I have tried to argue, the neutral state and the Christian nation go hand in hand. Neither do I plead for some "cultural" transmogrification of religion, some wishy-washy affection for our "roots." It is not a matter of remembering our roots! It is rather a matter of becoming aware of our political genesis and substance.

For the sake of contrast, just imagine what could happen if this middle dimension does not hold. First, Europe would crumble into more and more numerous and unrelated segments; second, its allegedly common institutions and its supposedly governing classes would lose themselves in a hollow representation of, and futile aspiration toward, a homogeneous and limitless human world. Our common capacity for human experience and a rational response to it would inevitably erode.

To strike the middle ground between the puny and the immense, the petty and the limitless, is not a matter of individual or even collective capacity or striving. You cannot produce it at will, as you can willingly let yourself slide toward the local and the mean, or as you can embark at will on the fabrication of whatever big institutional scheme has caught your imagination. A disposition of political things has come to pass, depending on the "historical contingency" to which I referred earlier. These political bodies— the nations—have nothing natural about them, even though, and I say this on good authority, man is by nature a political animal. The nations have resulted from our forebears' efforts to govern themselves under the unprecedented possibilities and constraints of the Christian dispensation. Only with the most strenuous exertion can we again become aware of these possibilities and constraints and their indirect but no less formative power. Currently, in the best of cases we find our nations to be like boring domestic animals, offering the comfort of their fur against the cold winds of globalization. They are for us only the puny, and we look with dread toward the immense. In truth, though, the European nations envelop the puny and the immense because they resulted from the effort to strike an unprecedented balance between the two, an effort made possible by the Christian affirmation. It is not that we have become too open-minded for our old national selves. It is rather that we are no longer able to grasp or even to feel the strength and delicacy of this balance.

INDEX

ABOUT THE AUTHOR AND TRANSLATOR

PIERRE MANENT teaches political philosophy in the Centre des recherches politiques Raymond Aron in Paris. His previous works in English include *An Intellectual History of Liberalism, Tocqueville and the Nature of Democracy, The City of Man,* and *A World beyond Politics? A Defense of the Nation-State.*

PAUL SEATON is associate professor of philosophy at St. Mary's Seminary and University in Baltimore. He cotranslated (with Daniel J. Mahoney) *Modern Liberty and Its Discontents,* a collection of Pierre Manent's work.